hamlyn
Quick**Cook**

hamlyn

QuickCook
Pasta

Recipes by Emma Lewis

Every dish, three ways – you choose!
30 minutes | 20 minutes | 10 minutes

An Hachette UK company
www.hachette.co.uk

First published in Great Britain in 2012 by Hamlyn,
a division of Octopus Publishing Group Ltd
Endeavour House, 189 Shaftesbury Avenue London WC2H 8JY
www.octopusbooks.co.uk

ISBN: 978-0-600-62369-4

A CIP catalogue record for this book is available from the British Library

Printed and bound in China

1 2 3 4 5 6 7 8 9 10

Both metric and imperial measurements are given for the recipes. Use one set of
measurements only, not a mixture of both.

Standard level spoon measurements are used in all recipes
1 tablespoon = 15 ml
1 teaspoon = 5 ml

Ovens should be preheated to the specified temperature. If using a fan-assisted
oven, follow the manufacturer's instructions for adjusting the time and temperature.
Grills should be preheated.

Eggs should be medium unless otherwise stated. The Department of Health advises
that eggs should not be consumed raw. This book contains some dishes made with
raw or lightly cooked eggs. It is prudent for more vulnerable people, such as pregnant
and nursing mothers, invalids, the elderly, babies and young children, to avoid
uncooked or lightly cooked dishes made with eggs.

This book includes dishes made with nuts and nut derivatives. It is advisable for those
with known allergic reactions to nuts and nut derivatives and those who may be
potentially vulnerable to these allergies, such as pregnant and nursing mothers,
invalids, the elderly, babies and children, to avoid dishes made with nuts and nut oils.
It is also prudent to check the labels of prepared ingredients for the possible inclusion
of nut derivatives.

Contents

Introduction

30 20 10 – Quick, Quicker, Quickest

This book offers a new and flexible approach to meal-planning for busy cooks, letting you choose the recipe option that best fits the time you have available. Inside you will find 360 dishes that will inspire and motivate you to get cooking every day of the year. All the recipes take a maximum of 30 minutes to cook. Some take as little as 20 minutes and, amazingly, many take only 10 minutes. With a bit of preparation, you can easily try out one new recipe from this book each night and slowly you will be able to build a wide and exciting portfolio of recipes to suit your needs.

How Does it Work?

Every recipe in the QuickCook series can be cooked one of three ways – a 30-minute version, a 20-minute version or a super-quick and easy 10-minute version. At the beginning of each chapter you'll find recipes listed by time. Choose a dish based on how much time you have and turn to that page.

You'll find the main recipe in the middle of the page accompanied by a beautiful photograph, as well as two time-variation recipes below.

If you enjoy the dish, you can go back and cook the other time options another time. If you liked the 20-minute Spaghetti Salsa Verde with Grilled Chicken, but only have 10 minutes to spare, then you'll find a way to cook it using cheat ingredients or clever shortcuts.

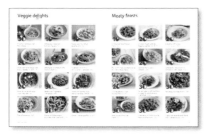

If you love the ingredients and flavours of the 10-minute Chorizo and Red Pepper Pasta, why not try something more substantial like the 20-minute Paella-style Red Pepper Pasta, or be inspired to cook a more elaborate version like a Pasta with Rich Red Papper Sauce. Alternatively, browse through all of the 360 delicious recipes, find something that takes your eye – then cook the version that fits your time frame.

Or, for easy inspiration, turn to the gallery on pages 12–19 to get an instant overview by themes, such as Veggie Delights or Meaty Feasts.

QuickCook online

To make life even easier, you can use the special code on each recipe page to email yourself a recipe card for printing, or email a text-only shopping list to your phone. Go to www.hamlynquickcook.com and enter the recipe code at the bottom of each page.

PAS-MIDW-QEC

QuickCook Pasta

For many years the story was that Marco Polo invented pasta when he tasted noodles on his travels to China and spread the word as soon as he returned to Italy. It's a lovely image, but historians think Europeans have been enjoying pasta for many years, certainly since Roman times. No doubt it's maintained its popularity because it's good value, quick to cook and can be enjoyed with so many different flavours. Even within Italy, you'll find plenty of variations. Northern Italy tends to favour rich sauces such as the famous ragu alla Bolognese or Genovese pesto, while the central zone favours simpler dishes like carbonara and amatriciana. In the South you'll find lighter sauces with plenty of olive oil, tomatoes and often a scattering of vegetables and seafood. From its homeland in Italy, a love of pasta has spread around the world. From new classics such as alfredo sauce or penne a la vodka, developed in USA to more exotic flavours found in Spanish or even Mexican inspired pasta dishes, to the classic child friendly macaroni cheese, you can find fast and satisfying dinners.

QuickCook Techniques and Tips

How to cook pasta

To start, you'll need your largest pan. Pasta needs a lot of water to cook in – at least 3 Litres (5½ pts) for 400 g (13 oz) pasta. Otherwise it not only won't cook evenly, but it tends to turn gummy. You will also need plenty of salt – the water should taste a little of the sea. This means adding about 1 tablespoon of salt to the pan. This will seem like a lot, but remember most of it will be drained away, leaving the pasta delicately flavoured. People often add some olive oil to the pan, but cooked properly, this isn't really necessary.

Make sure your water is brought to a very vigorous rolling boil over your highest heat setting. Add the pasta all in one go, so it cooks uniformly. Stir with a long spoon to help prevent sticking, then let it return to the boil. Leave to cook, stirring occasionally, and lowering the heat just a little if it threatens to boil over. Start timing from the moment the pan returns to the boil. The cooking time will depend on the type of pasta and the brand. Fresh pasta cooks in a matter of minutes, while some pastas made from high quality hard wheat take 15 minutes

How do you know it's done?

It's best to check the pasta about 2 minutes before the pack instructions suggest. It should be al dente which means 'to the tooth', soft and tender but with a little bite. You don't want overcooked mushy pasta which has lost all its chewy qualities. If it's underdone it will still have a chalky core and the slight taste of raw flour.

Draining

Have a colander to hand and when the pasta is ready, scoop out half a mugful of water (you might need this later on when adding the sauce), then drain straight away. Do not drain too thoroughly – the hot pasta keeps cooking making the water evaporate drying it out. It should remain slippery so it can be mixed with the sauce.

The final mixing together

Some people serve pasta and sauce separately, but to fully appreciate the flavours you need to toss them together. Tip the pasta back into the cooking pan and pour over the sauce. You want enough sauce to moisten but not drown or overwhelm the pasta. You will probably also need to add a couple of tablespoons of cooking water to the pan. Have some warmed bowls to hand and then serve straight away – remember pasta waits for no one.

QuickCook Ingredients/Storecupboard

A well-stocked larder is an asset to any kitchen, and is worth building up when you have time. The following ingredients are used in some of the recipes, especially the 10 minute variations, as sometimes 'ready-cooked' (meaning shop-bought) ingredients that can be bought for a reasonable price, are a sensible alternative to 'homemade'.

Jars of shop-bought tomato pasta sauce that can be used as a base, or on their own, are occassionally listed. Buy the best you can afford, preferably from the chiller cabinet or go for organic, with no added flavourings. Shop-bought roasted chicken breast fillets can be a reasonably priced alternative, and keep in the fridge for a few days. As for sauce additions, shop-bought cooked and peeled chestnuts keep for a long time in the cupboard and are surprisingly versatile. Shop-bought ready-cooked caramelized onion, and easy-fried onion which comes in a jar also both save time.

Where shop-bought red, green pesto and hummus are suggested, we mean the fresh pesto in containers, found in the deli section of your local supermarket. Experiment and you will find a supermarket-own brand that you like best. Sometimes we have suggested using packets of tortelloni or gnocchi as well as roasted red peppers from a jar, drained. Ready-cooked lentils in packs or cans, can speed up the cooking time, and avoids soaking overnight. Cans of tuna and sardines pack delicious tastes that are a good base for sauces.

Choosing the right pasta
Fresh or dry? People often spend more money on fresh pasta, but this isn't always the best option. Finding truly fresh pasta is a challenge, and making it is very time-consuming, so it can be better to choose a really good quality dry option. Italian ones are generally the best, probably because pasta manufacturers in Italy have to adhere to a strict set of guidelines. Choose pasta made from one hundred percent durum wheat. This is a very hard type of wheat and means the pasta will maintain its shape, texture and flavour well. It's using this type of flour which makes pasta different from other noodles as it's so malleable and can be twisted, stretched and pressed to make hundreds of different shapes. In addition to plain pasta you can also find golden egg pasta. This is silkier and smoother and works best with rich butter and cream-based sauces which come from the North of Italy while plain pasta is better with oil sauces more traditional in the South. If you are lucky enough to live near a specialist Italian shop which makes pasta in-house you can buy freshly rolled sheets of pasta. Unlike fresh lasagna sold pre-packaged in supermarkets, these will keep only for a day or two and are soft and malleable enough for you to make your own ravioli and tortelloni. They are a treat, cut into small strips, used in a lasagna. For the health conscious there is now a wide variety of pasta shapes made from whole wheat. This darker pasta is made from wholegrain flour which is healthier than white, refined flour but often will take longer to cook. In health food shops and the specialist aisle of supermarkets you'll also see lots of popular pasta shapes which are gluten-free and can be

eaten by those with wheat allergy. These are normally made from rice and maize flours and can be used instead of the regular wheat varieties. If you're feeling adventurous you can also find pasta coloured with vegetables and dyes – green spinach pasta, but purple beetroot is also good as are orange squash and deep black squid ink varieties.

Types of pasta

Just about every pasta shape that you could imagine exists, from novelty reindeer or tiny star shaped pasta for soup to classics like spaghetti. As a rule you can divide pasta into three types – filled pastas such as tortelloni, or their smaller cousins tortellini, ravioli and cannelloni tubes, long strands of pasta and short tubes and pasta shapes. While a lot depends on your preference (and what pasta you have in the house), for the best results you should try to match your sauce to the pasta you are using. As a general rule short tubes of pasta and pasta shapes are better at trapping in the flavours of chunky sauces, long strands are better paired with thinner delicate sauces.

The best known of these is of course spaghetti, but thicker linguine and thicker still, flat, tagliatelle are also popular as are the very thin strands called angel hair or capellini. If you want to try something different, look out for bucatini, thick hollow strands or pappardelle which are very broad ribbons.

Penne is an ever popular pasta tube along with the fatter rigatoni and kids favourite macaroni. You can also use shell shaped pasta such as conchiglie or very large tubes such as tubetti. Other dependable shapes include farfalle the pretty butterfly style and twists of fusilli. Artisin pastas are more popular like uneven thick trofie and the flat discs of orcchiette.

How much pasta

There is no firm rule on how much pasta to cook. In Italy pasta is normally served as part of a larger meal, while in other countries it's the main event. But a good rule of thumb is to allow about 100 g (3½ oz) of pasta per person for a main meal. The recipes in this book are easy to scale up or down for different numbers, and it's simple to add another handful to the pan if your dinners look a little hungry. Also, if you wish to use a fresh pasta where dried is suggested, scale the quantity up for fresh. More fresh pasta (roughly a third of the weight again) will be needed to make up the same finished amount.

Pasta bakes

Hearty and wholesome, these mouthwatering dishes make for the cosiest of meals.

Spicy Mushroom Rigatoni Bake 52

Chicken, Bacon and Asparagus Pasta Bake 86

Cheesy Tomato Pasta Bake 128

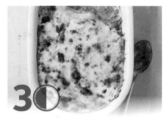

Ham and Courgette Lasagne 142

Pasta Rolls with Red Pepper and Ricotta 146

Broccoli and Ham Pasta Bake 164

Tuna and Sweetcorn Pasta Bake 168

Spinach and Ricotta Cannelloni 172

Hearty Sausage and Spinach Pasta Bake 174

Sin-Free Macaroni Cheese with Tomato 226

Blue Cheese and Cauliflower Cannelloni 258

Macaroni Prawn Gratin 266

Something a little bit different

Perfect for everyday eating, easy, unusual pasta dishes.

Individual Bacon Frittatas 32

Herby Fettucine with
Fried Eggs 38

Creamy Chicken and
Artichoke Frittata 62

Spanish Seafood Pasta 116

Farfalle with Chicken
Sweetcorn Bites and Red
Pepper Sauce 148

Seafood Spaghetti
in a Creamy Sauce 150

Frying Pan Macaroni
Cheese 160

Open Butternut Squash and
Ricotta Lasagne 188

Spiced Lentils with
Vermicelli 202

Creamy Vodka and
Tomato Taconelli 240

Salmon and Courgette
Pasta 242

Sweet Potato Pockets with
Sage Butter and Amaretti 278

Soups and salads

Light and healthy starters, mains and snacks.

Courgette, Pea and Pasta Soup with Pesto 24

Spicy Fish Soup 36

Greek Style Tomato, Olive and Feta Pasta salad 44

Salmon Pasta Salad with Dill Dressing 48

Fresh Herb Pasta Salad 50

Red Pepper Rocket and Parmesan Pasta salad 64

Classic Minestrone 132

No-chop Tomato and Rocket Pasta Salad 136

Tomato Soup with Pasta Shapes 140

Turkey Meatball and Pasta Soup 182

Pasta Nicoise 190

Light Clam and Tomato Broth 232

Spice up your spaghetti

The 10 minute staple is adaptable for all occasions.

Spaghettini with Tomato
and Basil Butter 68

Spaghetti with Watercress
Pesto and Blue Cheese 80

Creamy Anchovy, Lemon and
Rocket Spaghetti 88

Spaghetti Salsa Verde
with Grilled Chicken 94

Spaghetti Carbonara 130

Easy Sausage Spaghetti
Bolognese 158

Rocket, Chilli and Ricotta
Spaghetti 184

Spaghetti with Kale and
Gruyère 192

Spaghetti with Mini
Tuna Balls 206

Red Pepper and
Walnut Spaghetti 214

Spaghetti with Monkfish,
Mussels and Fennel 248

Fiery Black Spaghetti
with Squid 254

Fish and seafood

A medley of fresh fish dishes, for lunch and suppers.

Tuna and White Bean Pasta with Gremolata 70

Linguine with Seafood in a Tomato Sauce 92

Lemony Conchiglie with Tuna and Capers 100

Bucatini with Sardines and Fennel 112

Salmon and Leek Conchiglie 166

Gnocchi with Salmon in a Chilli Tomato Sauce 218

Linguine with Tuna Sashimi and Rocket 234

Zingy Crab Vermicelli 236

Seared Seabass with Warm Pasta Salad and Basil Oil 252

Pasta with Salmon, Rocket and Red Onion 268

Creamy Lobster Fettucine 270

Creamy Tomato Pasta with Prawns 274

Cheesy treats

Cheese-led pasta meals that are full of flavour.

Spaghetti with Beetroot and Goats' Cheese 26

Penne with Broccoli and Blue Cheese Sauce 34

Herby Goats' Cheese Pasta 46

Aubergine and Mozzarella Fusilli Lunghi 82

Creamy Gorgonzola Gnocchi 106

Linguine with Chicory, Pancetta and Mascarpone 108

Prawn, Tomato and Feta Rigatoni 110

Sweet Potato and Spinach Penne 120

Four-Cheese Pasta with Watercress Salad 134

Pea Fusili with Bacon and Ricotta 138

Conchiglie with Spinach and Goats' Cheese 196

Goats' Cheese and Sun-Dried Tomato Ravioli 244

Veggie delights

Meat-free pasta dishes, perfect for entertaining or feeding the family.

Creamy Chickpea and Pasta Soup 28

Artichoke, Olive and Lemon Linguine 30

Springtime Tortelloni with Ricotta 56

Chilli and Caper Tagliatelle with Ciabatta Crumbs 78

Aubergine and Mozzarella Fusilli Lunghi 82

Tagliarelle with Pesto and Charred Tomatoes 162

Fresh Pasta Broth with Onion Garnish 180

Mushroom Tagliatelle Bolognese 194

Fusilli with Lentils, Kale and Caramelized Onion 198

Pasta Primavera 208

Penne with Blackened Broccoli, Chilli and Garlic 224

Creamy Asparagus Pasta 262

Meaty feasts

Delicious meals, perfect for a balanced meal.

Chorizo and Red Pepper Pasta 90

Chicken Fusilli with Red Pepper and Almond Pesto 104

Linguine with Spicy Lamb Sauce 118

Pasta with Pork and Mushrooms in a White Wine Sauce 122

Chicken Fettuccine Alfredo 144

Chicken Parmigiana with Tomato Fusilli Lunghi 152

Creamy Mustard and Sausage Pasta 154

Lamb Cutlets with Garlicky Courgette and Anchovy Tagliatelle 246

Summery Sausage Pasta 250

Venison and Chestnut Sardi 256

Mafaldine with Rich Confit Duck and Pancetta 260

Tagliarelle with Seared Steak and Goulash Sauce 276

QuickCook

Light
Bites

Recipes listed by cooking time

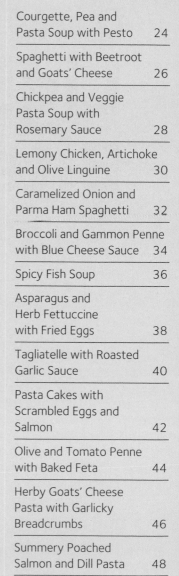

10

Courgette, Pea and Pasta Soup with Pesto

Serves 4

1 tablespoon olive oil
1 onion, finely chopped
50 ml (2 fl oz) dry white wine
1.5 litres (2½ pints) hot
    chicken stock
2 courgettes, chopped
125 g (4 oz) frozen peas
125 g (4 oz) macaroni
25 g (1 oz) crème fraîche
4 tablespoons shop-bought
    fresh green pesto
salt and pepper
crusty bread, to serve

- Heat the oil in a saucepan, add the onion and cook for 5 minutes until softened. Pour over the wine and bring to the boil, then cook until reduced by half. Add the stock and simmer for 5 minutes.

- Add the courgettes and cook for 5 minutes, then stir in the peas and cook for a further 2–3 minutes until tender.

- Meanwhile, cook the pasta in a large saucepan of salted boiling water according to the pack instructions until al dente. Drain and add to the soup with the crème fraîche, then simmer for 1 minute.

- Ladle into serving bowls, then drizzle a spoonful of the pesto on top of each. Serve with plenty of crusty bread.

10 Quick Courgette, Pea and Pasta Soup with Pesto Melt a little butter in a saucepan, add 3 chopped spring onions and cook for a minute until softened. Pour over 1.5 litres (2½ pints) hot chicken stock, then add 2 chopped courgettes and 125 g (4 oz) farfalline pasta and simmer for about 5 minutes or until the pasta is cooked through. Add 125 g (4 oz) frozen peas to the pan 2–3 minutes before the end of the cooking time and cook until tender. Serve drizzled with pesto as above.

30 Courgette, Pea and Pasta Soup with Mint Pesto Toasts Make the soup as above. Meanwhile, lightly toast 25 g (1 oz) hazelnuts. Place in a small food processor or blender with ½ deseeded and chopped chilli and a handful of mint leaves. Add a good squeeze of lemon juice and a little grated rind and whizz together. Blend in enough extra virgin olive oil to form a smooth pesto. Toast 4 slices of ciabatta bread, then spoon on the pesto and crumble over 75 g (3 oz) goats' cheese. Ladle the soup into serving bowls and serve with the toasts on top.

20 Spaghetti with Beetroot and Goats' Cheese

Serves 4

15 g (½ oz) butter
1 onion, finely sliced
250 g (8 oz) cooked beetroot, chopped
125 ml (4 fl oz) dry white wine
200 ml (7 fl oz) hot chicken or vegetable stock
400 g (13 oz) spaghetti
75 g (3 oz) firm goats' cheese log, cut into 4 thick slices
75 ml (3 fl oz) soured cream
salt and pepper
chopped dill, to garnish

- Heat the butter in a large saucepan, add the onion and cook for 5 minutes or until softened. Add the beetroot and wine and cook for a further 5 minutes or until the wine has reduced by half. Pour over the stock and simmer for 5 minutes.

- Meanwhile, cook the pasta in a large saucepan of salted boiling water according to the pack instructions until al dente. Place the goats' cheese slices on a baking sheet lined with foil. Cook under a preheated hot grill for 3 minutes or until golden brown.

- Stir the soured cream into the beetroot and season. Drain the pasta and spoon into serving bowls. Spoon over the beetroot sauce, top each with a slice of goats' cheese and serve sprinkled with dill.

---

10 Quick Beetroot and Goats' Cheese Spaghetti Cook 400 g (13 oz) spaghetti according to the pack instructions until al dente. Meanwhile, place 250 g (8 oz) chopped cooked beetroot and 125 g (4 oz) soft goats' cheese in a food processor or blender and whizz together to form a chunky sauce. Drain the pasta, reserving a little of the cooking water, and return to the pan. Stir through the sauce, adding a little cooking water to loosen, and serve with grated Parmesan cheese.

30 Beetroot Pasta Bites with Goats' Cheese Cook 250 g (8 oz) angel hair pasta according to the pack instructions. Drain, then cool under cold running water and drain again. Grate 150 g (5 oz) cooked beetroot into a large bowl, then mix together with the pasta and 1 beaten egg. Heat 1 tablespoon olive oil in a nonstick frying pan. Spoon in tablespoons of the pasta mixture and cook for 2 minutes, then turn over and cook for a further 2–3 minutes until golden. Remove from the pan and keep warm. Repeat with the rest of the mixture to make 8 pasta bites. Toss together 100 g (3½ oz) watercress, 1 tablespoon sherry vinegar, 3 tablespoons extra virgin olive oil and the grated rind of ½ lemon in a bowl. Top the pasta cakes with the salad and serve with 75 g (3 oz) soft goats' cheese crumbled over.

 # Creamy Chickpea and Pasta Soup

Serves 4

2 tablespoons olive oil
1 onion, chopped
1 garlic clove, crushed
rosemary sprig, leaves stripped,
  or a pinch of dried rosemary
1 teaspoon tomato purée
pinch of dried chilli flakes, plus
  extra to serve
2 x 400 g (13 oz) cans chickpeas,
  rinsed and drained
1.5 litres (2½ pints) hot
  chicken stock
150 g (5 oz) conchigliette pasta
salt and pepper
chopped flat-leaf parsley,
  to garnish
Parmesan cheese shavings,
  to serve

- Heat the oil in a large saucepan, add the onion and garlic and cook for 5 minutes until softened. Stir in the rosemary, tomato purée and chilli flakes. Tip in the chickpeas, then add the stock and simmer for about 12 minutes. Remove the pan from the heat.

- Remove half the chickpeas from the pan using a slotted spoon. Using a stick blender, whizz the remaining mixture to form a smooth soup and season.

- Add the pasta and reserved chickpeas to the soup, return to the heat and cook for a further 5–7 minutes or until the pasta is cooked through.

- Ladle into serving bowls and serve sprinkled with the parsley, Parmesan shavings and extra chilli flakes.

Quick Chickpea and Pasta Soup Place 150 g (5 oz) conchigliette, 2 rinsed and drained 400 g (13 oz) cans chickpeas and 1.5 litres (2½ pints) hot chicken stock in a large saucepan and simmer for 8 minutes until heated through and the pasta is cooked. Just before serving, stir in 5 tablespoons shop-bought red pepper hummus, then sprinkle with plenty of chopped flat-leaf parsley.

Chickpea and Veggie Pasta Soup with Rosemary Sauce Cook the onion and garlic as above, adding 1 chopped celery stick and 1 peeled and chopped carrot. Stir in the rosemary, tomato purée, chilli flakes, chickpeas and stock as above and simmer for about 12 minutes. Add the conchigliette to the pan 7 minutes before the end of the cooking time. Meanwhile, place the stripped leaves from 2 rosemary sprigs, 1 small bunch of flat-leaf parsley and 1 chopped garlic clove in a food processor or blender. Add a good squeeze of lemon juice and enough extra virgin olive oil to form a sauce. When the pasta is cooked through, ladle the soup into bowls and swirl over the rosemary sauce to serve.

Artichoke, Olive and Lemon Linguine

Serves 4

325 g (11 oz) linguine
125 g (4 oz) char-grilled artichoke
   hearts in oil, drained
3 tablespoons extra virgin
   olive oil
juice and grated rind of 1 lemon
75 g (3 oz) black olives
salt and pepper
chopped flat-leaf parsley,
   to garnish
Parmesan cheese shavings,
   to serve

- Cook the pasta in a large saucepan of salted boiling water according to the pack instructions until al dente. Drain, reserving a little of the cooking water.

- Return the pasta to the pan and stir through the remaining ingredients, adding a little cooking water to loosen if needed, and season.

- Spoon into serving bowls and serve sprinkled with the parsley and Parmesan shavings.

2 **Lemony Chicken, Artichoke and Olive Linguine** Heat a little olive oil in a frying pan. Add 2 boneless chicken breasts and 4 chopped bacon rashers and cook for 12–15 minutes, turning the chicken over once during cooking. Add 2 sliced spring onions and 1 sliced garlic clove and cook for a further 2 minutes until softened. Meanwhile, cook the linguine as above. Remove the chicken from the pan, discard the skin and cut into bite-sized pieces. Return to the pan and add the artichokes and black olives as above, a good squeeze of lemon juice and 3 tablespoons crème fraîche and heat through. Drain the pasta and return to the pan. Stir through the chicken mixture with a handful of chopped flat-leaf parsley. Serve at once.

3 **Artichoke, Olive and Lemon Frittata** Cook 200 g (7 oz) penne according to the pack instructions until al dente. Drain, then cool slightly under cold running water and drain again. Return to the pan and toss together with 6 beaten eggs, 125 g (4 oz) char-grilled artichoke hearts in oil, drained, and 75 g (3 oz) black olives. Stir in a handful of chopped mint leaves and the grated rind of 1 lemon. Heat a little olive oil in a large frying pan, pour in the egg mixture and cook over a low heat for 15 minutes until just set (you may have to finish off under the grill). Cut into wedges and serve.

 Individual Bacon Pasta Frittatas

Serves 4

6 streaky bacon rashers
325 g (11 oz) quick-cook spaghetti
5 eggs, beaten
125 ml (4 fl oz) single cream
50 g (2 oz) Gruyère cheese,
   grated
handful of flat-leaf parsley,
   chopped, to garnish
butter, for greasing
salt and pepper

• Cook the bacon under a preheated medium grill for 7 minutes until cooked through. Cool, then cut into small pieces.

• Meanwhile, cook the pasta in a large saucepan of salted boiling water according to the pack instructions until al dente. Drain, then cool under cold running water and drain again. Cut into 2.5 cm (1 inch) lengths.

• Mix together the eggs, cream and most of the cheese in a large bowl and season well. Stir in the cut pasta and bacon.

• Grease a 12-hole muffin tin. Spoon a little of the mixture into each hole until nearly to the top. Sprinkle over the remaining cheese, then place in a preheated oven, 200°C (400°F), Gas Mark 6, for 15–20 minutes or until the mixture is just set. Serve sprinkled with parsley.

Simple Bacon Spaghetti with Toasted Breadcrumbs

Cook 4 bacon rashers as above, then slice into small pieces. Meanwhile, cook the spaghetti as above. Heat a little olive oil in a frying pan, add 25 g (1 oz) fresh white breadcrumbs and cook until crisp. Drain the pasta and return to the pan. Stir through the bacon, 3 tablespoons crème fraîche and a handful of chopped basil leaves. Serve topped with the toasted breadcrumbs.

Caramelized Onion and Parma Ham Spaghetti Heat a little olive oil in a frying pan, add 1 sliced onion and 1 sliced garlic clove and cook over a low heat for 15–20 minutes until soft and golden. Meanwhile, cook the spaghetti as above. Drain well and return to the pan. Stir 2 tablespoons crème fraîche and 4 slices of Parma ham, cut into small strips, into the onions, then toss through the pasta. Serve immediately.

Penne with Broccoli and Blue Cheese Sauce

Serves 4

325 g (11 oz) penne
1 small head of broccoli, broken
   into florets
150 g (5 oz) creamy blue cheese,
   such as Gorgonzola or St Agur
50 ml (2 fl oz) single cream
salt and pepper

- Cook the pasta in a large saucepan of salted boiling water according to the pack instructions until al dente. Add the broccoli 5 minutes before the end of the cooking time and cook until tender.

- Meanwhile, place the cheese in a bowl and mash until smooth, then stir in the cream.

- Drain the pasta and broccoli, reserving a little of the cooking water, and return to the pan. Stir through the cheese mixture, adding a little cooking water to make a thin sauce if needed. Season well and serve immediately.

2 Broccoli and Gammon Penne with Blue Cheese Sauce
Brush a little oil over 2 thick gammon steaks and cook under a preheated medium grill for 5–7 minutes on each side. Leave to cool, then slice. Meanwhile, make the recipe as above, stirring the sliced gammon into the pasta with the cheese mixture. Serve immediately.

3 Broccoli, Blue Cheese and Penne Gratin Cook 400 g (13 oz) penne and the broccoli as above. Meanwhile, melt 50 g (2 oz) butter in a saucepan and stir in 50 g (2 oz) plain flour to make a smooth paste. Cook until golden, then gradually whisk in 500 ml (17 fl oz) milk and simmer for 5–10 minutes until thickened. Stir through 125 g (4 oz) chopped blue cheese. Drain the pasta and broccoli and mix together with the cheese sauce. Place in a heatproof dish and scatter over 125 g (4 oz) grated mozzarella cheese. Cook under a preheated medium grill for 5–10 minutes until golden and cooked through.

Spicy Fish Soup

Serves 4

2 tablespoons olive oil

1 garlic clove, sliced

1 red chilli, deseeded and finely chopped, plus extra sliced chilli to serve (optional)

½ teaspoon ground cumin

1 teaspoon paprika

1.5 litres (2½ pints) hot fish stock

400 g (13 oz) white fish, such as cod or haddock, skinned, boned and cut into bite-sized chunks

150 g (5 oz) stelline pasta

juice of ½ lemon

salt and pepper

coriander sprigs, to garnish

- Heat the oil in a large saucepan, add the garlic and chilli and cook for 30 seconds until beginning to turn golden. Stir in the cumin and paprika, then pour over the stock.

- Bring to the boil, then reduce the heat, season, add the fish and simmer for 5 minutes.

- Add the pasta and cook for a further 7–10 minutes until the fish and pasta are cooked through.

- Ladle into serving bowls and drizzle over the lemon juice to taste. Serve with sprigs of coriander and sliced chilli, if liked.

Tomato and Spicy Prawn Soup Place 300 ml (½ pint) shop-bought tomato pasta sauce and 750 ml (1¼ pints) hot fish stock in a saucepan and bring to the boil. Add the chilli, spices and stelline as above, then simmer for about 7 minutes until the pasta is cooked through. Add 150 g (5 oz) cooked peeled prawns to the pan 2 minutes before the end of the cooking time and cook until they are heated through. Serve immediately.

Spicy Baked Fish with Herby Linguine Rub a little olive oil over 4 thick cod fillets or other white fish fillets, place in an ovenproof dish and sprinkle with paprika and cumin. Leave to marinate for 5 minutes. Bake in a preheated oven, 190°C (375°F), Gas Mark 5, for 10–15 minutes until cooked through. Meanwhile, cook 300 g (10 oz) linguine according to the pack instructions until al dente. Drain, then cool under cold running water and drain again. Return to the pan and stir through 3 tablespoons extra virgin olive oil, a squeeze of lemon juice, 1 crushed garlic clove and a handful of chopped mint and coriander leaves. Serve alongside the baked fish.

Herby Fettuccine with Fried Eggs

Serves 4

300 g (10 oz) fettuccine
15 g (½ oz) Parmesan cheese,
  grated, plus extra to serve
handful of flat-leaf parsley,
  chopped, plus extra to garnish
3 tablespoons olive oil
1 garlic clove, finely chopped
4 eggs
pinch of dried chilli flakes
salt and pepper

- Cook the pasta in a large saucepan of salted boiling water according to the pack instructions until al dente. Drain, reserving a little of the cooking water, and return to the pan. Toss together with the Parmesan, parsley and a little cooking water to loosen. Season well.

- Meanwhile, heat the oil in a large nonstick frying pan, add the garlic and cook for a couple of seconds, then crack the eggs into the pan. Cook for 3 minutes so the whites are cooked through but the yolks are still runny.

- Spoon the pasta into serving bowls and top each with a fried egg. Serve scattered with the chilli flakes, extra chopped parsley and grated Parmesan.

2 Asparagus and Herb Fettuccine with Fried Eggs Toss 150 g (5 oz) trimmed asparagus spears in a little olive oil, then place on a grill rack. Cook under a preheated hot grill for 5 minutes until lightly charred, turning once, then cut into bite-sized pieces. Cook and drain the fettuccine as above. Meanwhile, heat a little olive oil in a frying pan and fry 4 quail eggs for 2 minutes until just cooked through. Toss the asparagus and a handful of chopped flat-leaf parsley through the pasta, then serve topped with the fried eggs and fresh Parmesan.

3 Sausage, Fried Egg and Herby Brunch Pasta Heat a little olive oil in a large frying pan, add 6 pork sausages and cook over a medium heat for 20 minutes or until cooked through. Remove the sausages from the pan, cool slightly and cut into bite-sized pieces. Add a handful of mushrooms, trimmed and halved, and cook for a further 1–2 minutes, then add 100 g (3½ oz) cherry tomatoes and cook until the tomatoes start to soften. Meanwhile, cook the fettuccine and fry 4 eggs as above. Drain the pasta and toss together with the sausages, mushrooms and tomatoes. Serve topped with a fried egg and sprinkled with chopped flat-leaf parsley and grated fresh Parmesan cheese.

10  Tagliatelle with Spicy Garlic Oil

Serves 4

125 ml (4 fl oz) extra virgin
olive oil
2 garlic cloves, sliced
½ red chilli, deseeded if liked,
and chopped
325 g (11 oz) spinach and
egg tagliatelle
salt and pepper
basil leaves, to garnish

- Pour the oil into a small saucepan, add the garlic and cook over a very low heat for 7 minutes or until the garlic starts to turn golden (if it turns black, you'll need to start again). Remove from the heat and add the chilli.

- Meanwhile, cook the pasta in a large saucepan of salted boiling water according to the pack instructions until al dente.

- Drain the pasta, reserving a little of the cooking water. Whisk 2 tablespoons of the cooking water into the garlic and chilli oil to make a smooth sauce, then season and toss through the pasta, adding a little more water if needed.

- Spoon on to serving plates and serve sprinkled with basil leaves.

---

20 **Tagliatelle with Roasted Garlic Sauce**
Place 8 garlic cloves, unpeeled, in a small roasting tin and toss in 2 tablespoons olive oil. Place in a preheated oven, 160°C (325°F), Gas Mark 3, for about 15 minutes or until soft. Squeeze the garlic out of their skins and mash together with 3 tablespoons crème fraîche in a bowl. Meanwhile, cook and drain the tagliatelle as above. Stir through the garlic sauce, adding a little cooking water to loosen if needed, and serve scattered with grated Parmesan cheese.

30 **Garlicky Onion Tagliatelle**
Heat a little olive oil in a frying pan, add 1 sliced onion and cook over a low heat for 20–25 minutes until softened and browned. Meanwhile, heat a knob of butter in a saucepan, add 3 sliced garlic cloves, 1 trimmed, cleaned and sliced leek, 1 sliced red onion and 3 sliced spring onions and cook gently for about 5 minutes until softened. Pour over 75 ml (3 fl oz) chicken stock and bubble for 5 minutes until the liquid has nearly cooked away. Meanwhile, cook and drain the tagliatelle as above. Toss through the garlicky onion mixture and the browned onion, then serve sprinkled with chopped chives and grated Pecorino cheese.

Pasta Cakes with Scrambled Eggs and Salmon

Serves 4

300 g (10 oz) angel hair pasta
6 tablespoons olive oil
4 eggs
3 tablespoons mascarpone cheese
handful of grated Parmesan cheese
4 slices of smoked salmon, cut into thin strips
salt and pepper
thinly sliced chives, to garnish

- Cook the pasta in a large saucepan of salted boiling water according to the pack instructions. Drain, then cool under cold running water and drain again. Tip into a bowl and toss through 1 teaspoon of the oil. Lightly beat 1 egg in a bowl and then mix together with the pasta.

- Heat a large nonstick frying pan, add half the remaining oil and curl the pasta into small cakes about 3 cm (1 inch) wide. Add about 4 of the pasta cakes to the pan and cook for 2 minutes, flattening the cakes down with the back of a spoon. Turn the cakes over and cook for a further 1 minute until golden all over. Remove from the pan and keep warm. Repeat with the remaining pasta cakes to make about 12.

- Crack the remaining 3 eggs into a small frying pan, dollop over the mascarpone and season well. Place over a low heat and cook for a couple of minutes until just beginning to set, then cook, gently stirring, for 3–5 minutes until creamy. Add the Parmesan and season well. Place 3 pasta cakes on each serving plate, spoon over a little scrambled egg and top with strips of smoked salmon. Serve sprinkled with chives.

1⓿ Easy Salmon Carbonara Cook 400 g (13 oz) angel hair pasta as above. Meanwhile, mix 2 tablespoons mascarpone and 1 beaten egg in a bowl. Drain the pasta, reserving a little of the cooking water, and return to the pan. Stir through the egg mixture and 4 slices of smoked salmon, cut into strips, adding a little cooking water to loosen if needed. Serve with extra mascarpone dolloped on top and sprinkled with chives as above.

3⓿ Pan-Fried Salmon with Creamy Asparagus Pasta Place the juice and grated rind of 1 lemon, 250 ml (8 fl oz) dry white wine and 1 bay leaf in a saucepan and bubble over a medium heat for 5–10 minutes until reduced. Pour in 250 ml (8 fl oz) double cream and cook for a further 5–10 minutes until reduced by half. Keep warm. Grind plenty of black pepper over 4 thin salmon steaks. Heat a little olive oil in a large frying pan, add the salmon and cook for 5 minutes on each side or until the fish is cooked and flakes easily. Meanwhile, cook 300 g (10 oz) linguine according to the pack instructions until al dente. Add 150 g (5 oz) asparagus tips to the pan 3 minutes before the end of the cooking time and cook until tender. Pass the sauce through a sieve, then season and mix in 1 egg yolk and a handful of chopped chives. Drain the pasta and asparagus and return to the pan. Stir through the sauce and serve alongside the salmon.

 # Greek-Style Tomato, Olive and Feta Pasta Salad

Serves 4

250 g (8 oz) cherry tomatoes, halved
4 tablespoons extra virgin olive oil
1½ tablespoons white wine vinegar
1 teaspoon oregano leaves, plus extra to garnish
1 teaspoon sugar
250 g (8 oz) penne
¼ cucumber, diced
75 g (3 oz) small black olives
75 g (3 oz) feta cheese, crumbled
salt and pepper

- Mix together the tomatoes and 2 tablespoons of the oil in a bowl, then place on a baking sheet. Drizzle over 1 tablespoon of the vinegar, sprinkle with the oregano and sugar and season well. Place in a preheated oven, 160°C (325°F), Gas Mark 3, for 20 minutes or until soft and starting to shrivel. Leave to cool slightly.

- Meanwhile, cook the pasta in a large saucepan of salted boiling water according to the pack instructions until al dente. Drain, then cool under cold running water and drain again. Tip into a serving dish and stir through the remaining oil and vinegar.

- Gently stir in the cucumber, olives and cooked tomatoes. Toss together and add the feta. Serve sprinkled with extra oregano leaves.

---

1 **Quick Olive, Rocket and Feta Pasta Salad**
Cook 300 g (10 oz) fresh penne according to the pack instructions until al dente, then drain as above. Tip into a serving dish and toss together with 75 g (3 oz) rocket leaves, 75 g (3 oz) pitted black olives, a squeeze of lemon juice and 1 tablespoon extra virgin olive oil. Serve scattered with 75 g (3 oz) crumbled feta cheese.

2 **Olive and Tomato Penne with Baked Feta** Heat a little olive oil in a saucepan, add 1 chopped onion and 2 finely chopped garlic cloves and cook until softened. Add 75 g (3 oz) pitted black olives and fry for a further 1–2 minutes. Stir in a 400 g (13 oz) can cherry tomatoes and bring to the boil. Reduce the heat, then simmer for 12 minutes until the sauce has thickened. Meanwhile, cook 300 g (10 oz) penne as above. Place 200 g (7 oz) feta cheese, in one piece, on a sheet of foil. Drizzle with olive oil and sprinkle with 1 teaspoon oregano leaves. Fold over the foil to make a parcel and place on a baking sheet. Bake in a preheated oven, 200°C (400°F), Gas Mark 6, for 10 minutes or until soft. Remove from the foil and cut into large pieces. Drain the pasta and return to the pan. Stir through the tomato sauce and serve topped with the baked cheese.

Herby Goats' Cheese Pasta

Serves 4

325 g (11 oz) fresh reginette pasta
150 g (5 oz) soft goats' cheese
handful of basil leaves, chopped,
  plus extra leaves to serve
  (optional)
handful of flat-leaf parsley,
  chopped, plus extra leaves to
  serve (optional)
handful of mint leaves, chopped,
  plus extra leaves to serve
  (optional)
salt and pepper

· Cook the pasta in a large saucepan of salted boiling water according to the pack instructions until al dente.

· Meanwhile, mash together the goats' cheese and herbs in a bowl and season lightly.

· Drain the pasta, reserving a little of the cooking water, and return to the pan. Stir through the herby cheese mixture, adding a little cooking water to loosen if needed. Spoon into bowls and serve sprinkled with extra herb leaves, if liked.

2 **Herby Goats' Cheese Pasta with Garlicky Breadcrumbs** Place 50 g (2 oz) ciabatta bread in a food processor or blender and whizz to form breadcrumbs. Transfer to a bowl and toss together with 2 tablespoons olive oil and 1 crushed garlic clove. Tip on to a baking sheet and cook under a preheated grill for a couple of minutes, turning often, until golden all over. Make the recipe as above, then serve scattered with the garlicky breadcrumbs.

3 **Tomato and Basil Pasta with Goats' Cheese** Heat 2 tablespoons olive oil in a saucepan, add 3 sliced garlic cloves and cook until softened. Tip in 2 x 400 g (13 oz) cans chopped tomatoes and simmer for 25 minutes until the sauce is very thick. Season well, then stir through a handful of chopped basil leaves. Meanwhile, cook and drain the reginette as above. Stir in the tomato and basil sauce and serve with 150 g (5 oz) soft goats' cheese crumbled on top.

1 Salmon Pasta Salad with Dill Dressing

Serves 4

350 g (11½ oz) fresh fusilli
2 spring onions, sliced
¼ cucumber, chopped
150 g (5 oz) smoked salmon,
  cut into strips

For the dill dressing

75 g (3 oz) crème fraîche
4 tablespoons mayonnaise
handful of dill, finely chopped
salt and pepper

- Cook the pasta in a large saucepan of salted boiling water according to the pack instructions until al dente. Drain the pasta, then cool under cold running water and drain again.

- Meanwhile, to make the dill dressing, mix together the crème fraîche, mayonnaise and dill in a bowl and season.

- Tip the pasta into a serving dish and stir through the spring onions, cucumber, smoked salmon and dill dressing.

---

2 Summery Poached Salmon and Dill Pasta Cut 1 fennel bulb into slices and place in a saucepan with a 400 g (13 oz) piece of salmon fillet. Pour over 100 ml (3½ fl oz) dry white wine, enough fish stock to cover and a couple of dill sprigs. Bring to the boil and then simmer for 10–12 minutes until the fish is cooked through and flakes easily. Remove the fish and fennel with a slotted spoon. Flake the fish into large chunks, removing any skin and bones, and keep warm with the fennel. Boil the poaching liquid until reduced down to 75 ml (3 fl oz), then stir through 3 tablespoons crème fraîche. Meanwhile, cook and drain the fusilli as above. Stir through the sauce, fennel and salmon. Sprinkle with a little chopped dill and serve immediately.

3 Salmon and Dill Frittata Cook 300 g (10 oz) spaghetti according to pack instructions until al dente. Drain, then cool under cold running water and drain again. Tip into a large bowl and mix together with 6 eggs, 150 g (5 oz) smoked salmon, cut into strips, and a good handful of chopped dill. Heat a frying pan, add 3 tablespoons olive oil and tip in the pasta mixture. Cook over a low heat for 15 minutes or until set. Cut into wedges, then serve dolloped with mascarpone cheese and sprinkled with extra chopped dill.

Fresh Herb Pasta Salad

Serves 4

200 g (7 oz) orzo
5 tablespoons extra virgin
  olive oil
juice of ½ lemon
2 spring onions, chopped
¼ cucumber, finely chopped
150 g (5 oz) tomatoes, chopped
large handful of flat-leaf parsley,
  chopped
small handful of mint leaves,
  chopped
salt and pepper

- Cook the pasta in a large saucepan of salted boiling water according to the pack instructions. Drain, then cool under cold running water and drain again.

- Tip into a serving dish and stir in the oil and lemon juice and season well. Toss through the remaining ingredients and serve.

1 **Simple Herby Pasta** Cook the orzo as above. Drain and return to the pan. Stir in 25 g (1 oz) butter, the chopped herbs as above and a squeeze of lemon juice. Serve immediately.

3 **Middle Eastern-Style Fresh Herb Pasta Salad** Make the pasta salad as above, adding a handful of pitted black olives, and arrange on a bed of chopped cos lettuce. Cut 2 round pitta breads in half horizontally (so they are very thin), then cut into wedges and place on a baking sheet. Drizzle with olive oil and sprinkle over paprika. Place in a preheated oven, 190°C (375°F), Gas Mark 5, for 5–10 minutes until just crisp. Leave to cool before scattering over the salad to serve.

 Spicy Mushroom Rigatoni Bake

Serves 2

300 g (10 oz) fresh rigatoni
2 tablespoons olive oil
1 garlic clove, finely sliced
½ red chilli, deseeded if liked,
   and chopped
150 g (5 oz) mixed mushrooms,
   preferably wild, trimmed and
   halved if large
grated rind of 1 lemon
handful of flat-leaf parsley,
   chopped
salt and pepper
grated Parmesan cheese,
   to serve

- Cook the pasta in a large saucepan of salted boiling water according to the pack instructions until al dente.

- Meanwhile, heat the oil in a frying pan, add the garlic, chilli and mushrooms and cook for a couple of minutes until the mushrooms colour slightly. Season well.

- Drain the pasta and return to the pan. Toss through the mushroom mixture and most of the lemon rind and parsley, reserving some for garnish.

- Place in a preheated oven, 200°C (400°F), Gas Mark 6, for 15 minutes or until golden, bubbling and cooked through.

- To serve, sprinkle over the reserved lemon rind and parsley and scatter with the Parmesan.

---

2 **Rigatoni with Baked Mushrooms**

Place 4 trimmed field mushrooms in an ovenproof baking dish. Dot over 25 g (1 oz) butter, season well and scatter over the leaves stripped from 1 thyme sprig. Place in a preheated oven, 180°C (350°F), Gas Mark 4, for 15 minutes. Remove from the oven and chop the mushrooms. Meanwhile, cook 200 g (7 oz) dried rigatoni according to the pack instructions until al dente. Drain and return to the pan, then stir through the chopped mushrooms with a squeeze of lemon juice. Serve immediately.

3 **Rigatoni with Mushroom and Blue Cheese Sauce** Heat a knob of butter and 1 tablespoon olive oil in a frying pan, add ½ thickly sliced onion and gently cook for 20 minutes until completely softened. Add 75 g (3 oz) mixed wild mushrooms, trimmed and halved if large, and cook for a further 3–5 minutes until softened. Mash together 60 g (2½ oz) Gorgonzola in a bowl until smooth and stir into the onion and mushrooms. Pour in 50 ml (2 fl oz) double cream and heat through. Meanwhile, cook 200 g (7 oz) dried rigatoni

according to the pack instructions until al dente. Drain and return to the pan, then stir through the sauce and serve sprinkled with chopped flat-leaf parsley.

Creamy Walnut Orecchiette

Serves 4

300 g (10 oz) fresh orecchiette
   pasta
salt and pepper
chopped basil leaves, to garnish

For the walnut paste

150 g (5 oz) walnuts
50 ml (2 fl oz) double cream
1 garlic clove, crushed
25 g (1 oz) Parmesan cheese,
   grated, plus extra to serve

• Cook the pasta in a large saucepan of salted boiling water according to the pack instructions until al dente.

• Meanwhile, make the walnut paste. Place the walnuts in a frying pan and dry-fry for a couple of minutes, shaking the pan every now and again, until toasted. Reserve some of the nuts for garnish and place the remainder in a food processor or blender. Add the cream, garlic and Parmesan, then whizz together to form a smooth paste.

• Drain the pasta, reserving a little of the cooking water, and return to the pan. Stir in the walnut paste, adding a little cooking water to loosen if needed. Season well.

• Spoon into serving bowls and serve scattered with the reserved walnuts, basil and extra Parmesan.

---

2 Walnut and Rocket Orecchiette with Crispy Breadcrumbs Put 75 g (3 oz) ciabatta bread in a food processor or blender and whizz to form breadcrumbs. Soak half the breadcrumbs in the 50 ml (2 fl oz) double cream for 5–10 minutes to soften. Make the walnut paste as above, adding the soaked breadcrumbs. Toss the remaining breadcrumbs in a little olive oil and toast in a frying pan until crisp. Meanwhile, cook and drain the orecchiette as above. Stir in the walnut sauce, adding a little cooking water to loosen if needed. Season, stir in a handful of rocket leaves and top with crispy breadcrumbs.

3 Crispy Chicken and Walnut Orecchiette Cook 300 g (10 oz) dried orecchiette according to the pack instructions until al dente. Make the walnut paste as above, adding 5 tablespoons chicken stock to form a thin sauce. Pour into a large saucepan and heat through. Tear 2 shop-bought roasted chicken breasts into strips, discarding the skin, and stir through the sauce. Drain the pasta and stir into the sauce with 2 sliced spring onions, a pinch of paprika and a little chopped dill. Tip into a large heatproof dish. Cover with 50 g (2 oz) fresh white breadcrumbs, drizzle with olive oil and cook under a preheated medium grill for 5–10 minutes or until cooked through.

Springtime Tortelloni with Ricotta

Serves 2

250 g (8 oz) pack spinach and
   ricotta tortelloni
75 g (3 oz) frozen broad beans
75 g (3 oz) frozen peas
grated rind of 1 lemon
1 tablespoon extra virgin olive oil
50 g (2 oz) ricotta cheese
salt
handful of mint leaves, chopped,
   to garnish

- Cook the pasta in a large saucepan of salted boiling water according to the pack instructions. Add the broad beans 3–4 minutes and the peas 2–3 minutes before the end of the cooking time and cook until tender. Drain the pasta and vegetables and return to the pan.

- Stir through the lemon rind and olive oil. Spoon into serving bowls and serve topped with the ricotta and mint.

2 **Tortelloni with Pancetta and Ricotta** Heat a little olive oil in a frying pan, add 2 sliced spring onions and cook until softened. Add 100 g (3½ oz) pancetta cubes and cook gently for 7–10 minutes until lightly browned, then stir in a splash of dry white wine and cook until reduced down. Meanwhile, cook and drain the tortelloni as above. Stir through the pancetta and serve topped with the ricotta and mint as above.

3 **Tomato and Ricotta Tortelloni Bake** Cook a 250 g (8 oz) pack tortelloni for 1 minute less than directed on the pack instructions. Drain well and arrange half over the bottom of an ovenproof dish. Pour over 75 ml (3 fl oz) shop-bought tomato pasta sauce, then scatter over 50 g (2 oz) ricotta cheese. Add another layer of tortelloni and tomato sauce. Top with 75 g (3 oz) ricotta cheese, 50 g (2 oz) sliced mozzarella cheese and a small handful of grated Parmesan cheese. Place in a preheated oven, 190°C (375°F), Gas Mark 5, for 15–20 minutes until golden and heated through.

Bacon, and Tomato Tortiglioni with Mascarpone Mayonnaise

Serves 4

1 tablespoon olive oil
4 streaky bacon rashers
150 g (5 oz) cherry tomatoes
   on the vine
325 g (11 oz) tortiglioni
50 g (2 oz) rocket leaves

**For the mascarpone
  mayonnaise**

1 egg yolk
125 g (4 oz) mascarpone cheese
50 ml (2 fl oz) extra virgin
   olive oil
15 g (½ oz) Parmesan cheese,
   grated
salt and pepper

- Rub the oil on to a grill pan, add the bacon and cook under a preheated medium grill for 5–7 minutes until starting to crisp. Add the tomatoes. Shake the pan to coat in the oil, season and return to the grill. Cook for 5 minutes or until the bacon is cooked through and tomatoes are lightly charred. Meanwhile, cook the pasta in a saucepan of salted boiling water according to the pack instructions until al dente.

- To make the mascarpone mayonnaise, place the egg yolk and mascarpone together in a food processor and whizz together. With the motor still running, add the oil through the funnel, one small drop at a time, until you get a smooth mayonnaise-like sauce. Stir in the Parmesan and season.

- Drain the pasta, reserving a little cooking water, and return to the pan. Stir through a little of the mascarpone mixture, followed by the rocket. Add a little cooking water to loosen if needed. Spoon into bowls, dollop over the remaining mayonnaise and top with the bacon slices and tomato.

1 Quick Tomato, Parma Ham and Rocket Spaghettini Cook 325 g (11 oz) spaghettini in a large saucepan of salted boiling water according to the pack instructions until al dente. Drain, then return to the pan. Stir through 3 tablespoons mascarpone cheese mixed with 15 g (½ oz) grated Parmesan cheese, 4 drained and chopped sun-dried tomatoes in oil and 4 slices of Parma ham, cut into strips. Serve sprinkled with plenty of chopped rocket leaves.

3 Bacon, Tomato and Rocket Pasta Soufflés Cook the bacon as above. Meanwhile, cook 250 g (8 oz) quick-cook spaghetti according to the packet instructions until al dente. Melt 25 g (1 oz) butter in a large saucepan and stir in 25 g (1 oz) plain flour to make a smooth paste. Cook until golden, then gradually whisk in 300 ml (½ pint) milk and simmer, stirring regularly, for 5 minutes until thickened. Lift off the heat and stir through 25 g (1 oz) grated Parmesan cheese and 3 egg yolks. Whisk 3 egg whites in a clean bowl until stiff peaks form. Drain the pasta, slice into 2.5 cm (1 inch) lengths and chop the bacon, then add to the cheese sauce with 2 drained and chopped sun-dried tomatoes and a handful of rocket leaves, finely chopped. Gently stir in the whisked egg whites in three stages. Spoon into 4 individual greased soufflé dishes and place in a preheated oven, 200°C (400°F) Gas Mark 6, for 20 minutes or until golden and just cooked through.

PAS-LITE-RAV

Pasta Puttanesca

Serves 4

3 tablespoons olive oil
2 garlic cloves, sliced
½ teaspoon dried chilli flakes
8 anchovy fillets in oil, drained
2 x 400 g (13 oz) cans chopped
   tomatoes
125 g (4 oz) black olives
1 tablespoon capers, rinsed and
   drained
300 g (10 oz) pappardelle
salt and pepper
torn basil leaves, to garnish

- Heat the oil in a large saucepan, add the garlic, chilli flakes and anchovies and cook, stirring frequently, for a couple of minutes until the anchovies begin to disintegrate.

- Stir in the tomatoes and cook, fairly vigorously, for 15 minutes or until the sauce has thickened. Add the olives and capers and season.

- Meanwhile, cook the pasta in a large saucepan of salted boiling water according to the pack instructions until al dente. Drain and toss through the sauce.

- Spoon into serving bowls and serve sprinkled with the basil.

1 **Pappardelle with a No-Cook Caper and Olive Sauce** Cook and drain the pappardelle as above. Meanwhile, mix together 1 crushed garlic clove and 3 tablespoons extra virgin olive oil in a bowl. Roughly chop 1 large tomato and stir into the dressing with 2 teaspoons rinsed and drained capers and a handful of pitted black olives. Drain the pasta and return to the pan. Stir through the sauce and serve immediately.

3 **Chicken Pappardelle with Caper and Olive Dressing** Cook 4 boneless chicken breasts under a preheated hot grill for 7 minutes on each side or until golden and cooked through. Cook and drain the pappardelle as above, then stir through 350 ml (12 fl oz) shop-bought tomato pasta sauce. Heat 3 tablespoons olive oil in a small frying pan, add a handful of pitted black olives and cook for 1–2 minutes until beginning to sizzle.

Add 1 tablespoon rinsed and drained capers and cook for 30 seconds. Stir in 2 tablespoons chopped flat-leaf parsley and a squeeze of lemon juice. Arrange the pasta and slice and arrange the chicken on serving plates. Spoon over the warm dressing and serve.

30 Creamy Chicken and Artichoke Frittata

Serves 4

325 g (11 oz) spaghetti
6 eggs
100 g (3½ oz) crème fraîche
2 shop-bought roasted chicken
   breasts
25 g (1 oz) Parmesan cheese,
   grated
175 g (6 oz) artichoke hearts in
   oil or brine, drained and cut
   into wedges
2 spring onions, sliced
handful of basil leaves, chopped
small handful of mint leaves,
   chopped
2 tablespoons olive oil
salt and pepper

- Cook the pasta in a saucepan of salted boiling water according to the pack instructions until al dente.

- Meanwhile, whisk together the eggs and crème fraîche in a large bowl and season well. Tear the chicken into shreds, discarding the skin, and mix in with the Parmesan, artichokes, spring onions, basil and mint.

- Drain the pasta, then cool slightly under cold running water and drain again. Mix together with the egg mixture and season well.

- Heat a large nonstick frying pan over a medium heat, then add the oil. Tip in the pasta mixture, smoothing over the surface with a spoon. Leave to cook over a medium heat for 20 minutes until just set. Serve cut into wedges.

---

10 Quick Chicken and Artichoke Spaghetti Cook the spaghetti as above. Meanwhile, tear the chicken breasts into shreds as above and quarter the artichoke hearts. Drain the pasta, reserve a little of the cooking water, and return to the pan. Stir through the chicken, artichokes, a dollop of mascarpone cheese and a handful of grated Parmesan cheese, adding a little cooking water to loosen if needed. Serve at once.

20 **Griddled Chicken and Artichoke Pasta Salad** Season 2 boneless chicken breasts and cook on a preheated hot griddle for 7 minutes on each side or until cooked through. Meanwhile, cook 300 g (10 oz) fusilli according to the pack instructions until al dente. Drain, then cool under cold running water and drain again. Tip into a serving dish and toss together with the juice of ½ lemon and 3 tablespoons extra virgin olive oil. Tear the chicken into shreds, discarding the skin, and mix into the salad with the artichoke hearts as above, cut into chunks, and a handful of chopped mint leaves.

30 Red Pepper, Rocket and Parmesan Pasta Salad

Serves 4

4 tablespoons extra virgin
   olive oil
1 garlic clove, finely chopped
1 red chilli, deseeded and
   finely chopped
4 red peppers, cored, deseeded
   and cut into wedges
325 g (11 oz) gigli pasta
1 tablespoon white balsamic
   vinegar
75 g (3 oz) rocket leaves
handful of Parmesan cheese
   shavings
salt and pepper

· Heat 2 tablespoons of the olive oil in a frying pan, add the garlic and chilli and cook for 30 seconds. Add the red peppers and cook over a low heat for 20–25 minutes or until very soft. Leave to cool slightly.

· Meanwhile, cook the pasta in a large saucepan of salted boiling water according to the pack instructions until al dente. Drain, then rinse under cold running water until warm and drain again. Tip into a serving dish.

· Toss through the remaining oil, balsamic vinegar, rocket and the red peppers with all their cooking juices and season. Serve scattered with the Parmesan.

1 Pasta with Quick Roasted Red Pepper Sauce Cook and drain the gigli as above. Meanwhile, place 2 drained roasted red peppers from a jar, 1 crushed garlic clove and 125 g (4 oz) ricotta cheese in a food processor or blender and whizz together to form a creamy sauce. Drain the pasta, reserving a little of the cooking water, and return to the pan. Stir through the red pepper sauce, adding a little cooking water to loosen if needed, and a handful of chopped basil leaves. Serve immediately.

2 Spicy Red Pepper Pasta Cut 4 cored and deseeded red peppers into thin strips. Heat a little olive oil in a frying pan, add the red pepper strips and cook gently for 15 minutes until softened. Meanwhile, cook and drain the gigli as above. Place 3 deseeded tomatoes, 1 chopped spring onion and 1 halved and deseeded red chilli in a food processor or blender and whizz together to form a chunky sauce. Drain the pasta and return to the pan. Stir through the tomato sauce, 3 tablespoons olive oil and the cooked peppers. Serve immediately.

30 Fusilli Amatriciana with Pancetta

Serves 4

2 tablespoons olive oil

1 red chilli, deseeded if liked, and finely chopped

250 g (8 oz) pancetta slices, cut into strips

1 onion, finely chopped

1 rosemary sprig, leaves stripped and chopped

100 ml (3½ fl oz) fruity red wine

400 g (13 oz) can chopped tomatoes

200 ml (7 fl oz) water

400 g (13 oz) fusilli

salt and pepper

grated Parmesan cheese, to serve

- Heat a frying pan until hot, add the oil, chilli and pancetta and cook until beginning to crisp. Add the onion and rosemary and cook for a further 3–5 minutes until lightly coloured.

- Pour over the wine and bubble until reduced by half, then add the tomatoes and the measurement water and leave to simmer for at least 20 minutes until thickened. Season well.

- Meanwhile, cook the pasta in a large saucepan of salted boiling water according to the pack instructions until al dente. Drain and return to the pan, then toss through the sauce.

- Spoon into serving bowls and serve scattered with the Parmesan cheese.

1 **Fusilli with Parma Ham and Cherry Tomatoes** Cook and drain the fusilli as above. Toss through 150 g (5 oz) halved cherry tomatoes, a squeeze of lemon juice, 2 tablespoons crème fraîche and 100 g (3½ oz) thinly sliced Parma ham, cut into small strips. Serve immediately.

2 **Bacon and Sun-Dried Tomato Fusilli** Heat a little butter in a frying pan, add 1 trimmed, cleaned and sliced leek and cook for 5 minutes until beginning to soften. Cut 4 bacon rashers into small strips, add to the pan with 2 sliced spring onions and cook for a further 5 minutes. Pour over 25 ml (1 fl oz) dry white wine and cook for 3 minutes until reduced. Stir in 3 drained and chopped sun-dried tomatoes in oil and 4 tablespoons crème fraîche. Meanwhile, cook and drain the fusilli as above, then toss through the sauce. Serve at once.

 # Spaghettini with Tomato and Basil Butter

Serves 4

75 g (3 oz) butter, softened
5 sunblush tomatoes in oil,
   drained and finely chopped
handful of basil leaves, finely
   chopped,
grated rind of 1 lemon
325 g (11 oz) spaghettini
salt

- Mix together the butter, sunblush tomatoes, basil and lemon rind in a bowl and season well. Place on a sheet of clingfilm and roll up tightly to form a cylinder. Place in the freezer for 5 minutes to firm. (You can also make this ahead of time and store in the fridge or freezer until ready to use.)

- Meanwhile, cook the pasta in a large saucepan of salted boiling water according to the pack instructions until al dente. Drain well and pile on to serving plates.

- Cut slices of the flavoured butter, place on top of the pasta and serve immediately.

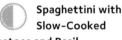 **Tomato and Basil Spaghettini with a Buttery Sauce** Heat a little butter in a saucepan, add 1 finely chopped shallot and cook for a couple of minutes until softened. Pour over 150 ml (¼ pint) dry white wine and cook for about 10 minutes until reduced. Cut 25 g (1 oz) cold butter into small chunks and whisk into the sauce one chunk at a time. Meanwhile, cook and drain the spaghettini as above. Stir through a handful of drained and chopped sunblush tomatoes in oil and a handful of chopped basil leaves and serve with the buttery sauce drizzled over.

Spaghettini with Slow-Cooked Tomatoes and Basil Cut 20 small tomatoes in half and arrange on a baking sheet. Drizzle over 3 tablespoons olive oil, 1 tablespoon balsamic vinegar and 1 teaspoon sugar. Place in a preheated oven, 160°C (325°F), Gas Mark 3, for 25–30 minutes until softened and lightly browned. Meanwhile, cook and drain the spaghettini as above. Toss through the tomatoes, a little more balsamic vinegar, a knob of butter and a handful of basil leaves and serve with 125 g (4 oz) soft goats' cheese crumbled over.

Tuna and White Bean Pasta with Gremolata

Serves 4

75 ml (3 fl oz) single cream
400 g (13 oz) can cannellini beans, rinsed and drained
225 g (7½ oz) can tuna in oil, drained
325 g (11 oz) ferretto pasta
salt and pepper

For the gremolata

1 garlic clove
grated rind of 1 lemon
handful of flat-leaf parsley, chopped

· Place the cream and beans in a saucepan and cook for 15 minutes or until the beans are very soft, adding a little water if needed. Stir the tuna into the sauce.

· Meanwhile, cook the pasta in a large saucepan of salted boiling water according to the pack instructions until al dente.

· To make the gremolata, place the garlic, lemon rind and parsley on a board and chop until fine but not mushy.

· Drain the pasta, reserving a little of the cooking water. Mix together the pasta and tuna sauce, adding a little cooking water to loosen if needed.

· Spoon into serving bowls and serve scattered with the gremolata.

---

1 Quick Tuna and White Bean Penne

Cook 400 g (13 oz) fresh penne according to the packet instructions until al dente. Add the cannellini beans as above to the pan 2 minutes before the end of the cooking time. Drain and return to the pan. Stir through 2 tablespoons crème fraîche, the grated rind of 1 lemon, the tuna as above and a handful of chopped flat-leaf parsley. Serve immediately.

3 Griddled Tuna with Creamy White Bean Pasta Heat a little olive oil in a saucepan, add 1 chopped onion and 1 crushed garlic clove and cook until softened. Add the cannellini beans and cream as above and a strip of orange and lemon rind and simmer for 15 minutes until really soft and creamy. Remove the rind and season. Meanwhile, cook and drain the ferretto as above, then add to the beans.

Rub a little black pepper and olive oil over 4 tuna steaks. Heat a griddle pan until smoking, add the tuna and cook for 3–5 minutes on each side or until browned on the outside but still rare inside. Spoon the creamy bean pasta into bowls, place the steaks on top and serve sprinkled with chopped flat-leaf parsley.

QuickCook

Midweek Meals

Recipes listed by cooking time

30

20

10

1 Creamy Asparagus, Pea and Lemon Pasta

Serves 4

500 g (1 lb) fresh cavatappi pasta
100 g (3½ oz) frozen peas
150 g (5 oz) thin asparagus tips
juice and grated rind of 1 lemon
125 g (4 oz) mascarpone cheese
2 tablespoons extra-virgin
   olive oil
salt and pepper
chopped basil leaves, to garnish

• Cook the pasta in a large saucepan of salted boiling water according to the pack instructions until al dente. Add the peas and asparagus 3 minutes before the end of the cooking time and cook until tender.

• Meanwhile, mix together most of the grated lemon rind and the mascarpone in a bowl.

• Drain the pasta and vegetables, reserving a little of the cooking water. Set aside the asparagus and keep warm, and return the pasta and peas to the pan. Stir through the lemon juice and oil, loosening with a little cooking water.

• Season well and spoon into serving bowls. Sprinkle with the basil and the rest of the zest, top with the asparagus and serve with a dollop of the lemon mascarpone in each dish.

2 Asparagus and Pea Spirali with Lemon Sauce
Cook 400 g (13 oz) spirali according to the pack instructions until al dente, adding the vegetables to the pan as above. Meanwhile, melt 25 g (1 oz) butter in a saucepan and stir in 3 tablespoons plain flour to make a smooth paste. Cook until golden, then gradually whisk in 100 ml (3½ fl oz) milk and 100 ml (3½ fl oz) double cream. Simmer for 5 minutes until thickened, then stir through the grated rind of 1 lemon and a handful of chopped basil leaves. Drain the pasta and vegetables and return to the pan, then stir through the sauce. Serve at once.

3 Asparagus, Pea and Lemon Spirali en Papillote
Cook 400 g (13 oz) spirali for 2 minutes less than directed on the pack instructions, adding the vegetables to the pan as above, then drain. Cut out 4 large pieces of nonstick baking paper and divide the drained pasta and vegetables between them. Squeeze over the juice of 1 lemon and pour over 50 ml (2 fl oz) hot chicken stock. Fold over the baking paper to seal the parcels and place on a baking sheet. Place in a preheated oven, 180°C (350°F), Gas Mark 4, for 10 minutes or until heated through. Open the parcels, spoon 1 tablespoon mascarpone cheese over each and serve topped with a slice of Taleggio cheese.

Chilli and Caper Tagliatelle with Ciabatta Crumbs

Serves 4

3 slices of ciabatta bread
75 ml (3 fl oz) olive oil
4 garlic cloves
1 red chilli, deseeded if liked, and finely sliced
2 tablespoons capers, rinsed and drained
400 g (13 oz) tagliatelle
juice and grated rind of 1 lemon
salt and pepper

- Place the ciabatta in a small food processor or blender and whizz to form coarse breadcrumbs. Pour the oil into a small frying pan and add the garlic. Cook over a low heat for about 10 minutes until a deep golden colour, then remove the cloves with a slotted spoon and discard. Add the breadcrumbs to the pan and cook for a further couple of minutes until beginning to colour. Remove the breadcrumbs with a slotted spoon and set aside. Add the chilli and capers and cook for 2 minutes until lightly browned.

- Meanwhile, cook the pasta in a large saucepan of salted boiling water according to the pack instructions until al dente. Drain, reserving a little of the cooking water, and return to the pan. Stir in the flavoured oil, lemon rind and juice and a little cooking water if needed. Season well.

- Spoon into serving bowls and serve scattered with the breadcrumbs.

---

1 **Easy Chilli, Caper and Tomato Tagliatelle** Cook and drain the tagliatelle as above and toss with the chilli and capers as above, 3 drained and chopped sunblush tomatoes in oil and 100 g (3½ oz) halved cherry tomatoes. Add a squeeze of lemon juice and top with plenty of rocket leaves. Serve immediately.

3 **Chilli and Caper Tagliatelle Parcels with Crispy Breadcrumbs** Cook the tagliatelle for 2 minutes less than directed on the pack instructions. Drain well and divide between 4 large squares of foil. Mix together a squeeze of lemon juice, 1 crushed garlic clove and the olive oil, chilli and capers as above and spoon over the pasta. Lift up the edges of the foil and fold over to seal, then place on a baking sheet.

Cook in a preheated oven, 180°C (350°F), Gas Mark 4, for 10 minutes or until cooked through. Whizz the ciabatta slices as above to make bread-crumbs, then toss in a little olive oil and toast in a frying pan until crisp. Tear open the parcels with a knife and sprinkle over a handful of chopped basil leaves. Dollop over a little crème fraîche and scatter over the crispy breadcrumbs. Serve immediately.

1 Spaghetti with Watercress Pesto and Blue Cheese

Serves 2

200 g (7 oz) wholewheat
  spaghetti
50 g (2 oz) blue cheese,
  thickly sliced
salt and pepper

For the watercress pesto

50 g (2 oz) walnuts
75 g (3 oz) watercress, plus extra
  sprigs to garnish
1 tablespoon crème fraîche

- Cook the pasta in a large saucepan of salted boiling water according to the pack instructions until al dente.

- Meanwhile, make the watercress pesto. Tip the walnuts into a small frying pan and dry-fry over a medium heat for 3 minutes, giving the pan a shake every now and again, until they start to turn brown. Leave to cool for a minute or two. Place the nuts, watercress and crème fraîche in a small food processor or blender and whizz together to form a pesto. Season well.

- Drain the pasta, then spoon into serving bowls and arrange slices of the cheese on top. Serve with dollops of the pesto and garnished with watercress sprigs.

---

2 Leek, Onion and Blue Cheese Spaghetti with Watercress

Toss a handful of small shallots and 150 g (5 oz) baby leeks, trimmed and cleaned, in a little oil. Place on a baking sheet and roast in a preheated oven, 200°C (400°F), Gas Mark 6, for 20 minutes or until softened and lightly browned. Meanwhile, cook and drain the spaghetti as above. Stir through the baked shallots and leeks, 150 g (5 oz) chopped blue cheese and 2 tablespoons crème fraîche. Serve topped with a handful of watercress.

3 Gnocchi with Blue Cheese and Watercress Pesto
Make the watercress pesto as above. Cook 250 g (8 oz) pack fresh gnocchi according to the pack instructions. Drain well and return to the pan. Stir through the watercress pesto, adding an extra 2 tablespoons crème fraîche, 3 tablespoons milk and 50 g (2 oz) chopped blue cheese. Place 1 slice of white bread and a handful of walnuts in a small food processor or blender to form breadcrumbs. Spoon the gnocchi into a heatproof dish, scatter with the breadcrumbs and cook under a preheated medium grill for 10 minutes or until golden and bubbling.

Aubergine and Mozzarella Fusilli Lunghi

Serves 4

4 tablespoons olive oil
1 aubergine, thickly sliced
300 ml (½ pint) shop-bought
    tomato pasta sauce
½ teaspoon dried chilli flakes
400 g (13 oz) fusilli lunghi
25 g (1 oz) Parmesan
    cheese, grated
125 g (4 oz) mozzarella
    cheese, cubed
salt and pepper
basil leaves, to garnish

- Heat half the oil in a large nonstick frying pan, add half the aubergine and cook for 5–7 minutes until softened and lightly golden. Season well, then remove from the pan to a plate. Repeat with the remaining oil and aubergine.

- Place the tomato pasta sauce and chilli flakes in a saucepan, add the cooked aubergine and simmer for a couple of minutes.

- Meanwhile, cook the pasta in a large saucepan of salted boiling water according to the pack instructions until al dente. Drain, reserving a little of the cooking water, and return to the pan. Stir through the aubergine sauce, adding a little cooking water to loosen if needed.

- Toss through the Parmesan and season, then spoon into serving bowls. Top with the mozzarella and serve sprinkled with the basil.

1 0 Simple Aubergine and Mozzarella Fusilli Cut 200 g (7 oz) aubergine into thin slices, rub with olive oil and season well. Cook under a preheated hot grill for 3–5 minutes on each side. Meanwhile, cook 400 g (13 oz) fusilli according to the pack instructions until al dente. Drain, reserving a little cooking water, and return to the pan. Toss through 5 tablespoons shop-bought fresh green pesto, mix in 125 g (4 oz) cubed mozzarella cheese and the grilled aubergine, adding a little cooking water to loosen if needed. Scatter with 25 g (1 oz) toasted pine nuts.

3 0 Fusilli Lunghi with Rich Aubergine Sauce and Mozzarella Prick 2 aubergines with a fork, place on a baking sheet and bake in a preheated oven, 220°C (425°F), Gas Mark 7, for 20 minutes or until soft and lightly charred. Leave to cool for 5 minutes, then peel away the skin. Crush 1 garlic clove in a small bowl and stir together with 3 tablespoons crème fraîche. Place in a food processor or blender with the aubergine flesh, a squeeze of lemon juice and a handful of chopped coriander leaves and whizz together to form a sauce. Meanwhile, cook and drain the fusilli lunghi as above. Stir through the aubergine sauce and serve topped with the mozzarella as above.

20 Ligurian Potato and Green Bean Pasta with Pesto

Serves 4

300 g (10 oz) trofie pasta
6 new potatoes, scrubbed
   and halved
125 g (4 oz) green beans, trimmed
salt and pepper

For the pesto

75 g (3 oz) basil leaves
25 g (1 oz) toasted pine nuts, plus
   extra to serve
1 garlic clove, crushed
100 ml (3½ fl oz) extra-virgin
   olive oil
3 tablespoons grated Parmesan
   cheese, plus extra to serve

- Cook the pasta in a large saucepan of salted boiling water according to the pack instructions until al dente.

- Meanwhile, cook the potatoes in a large saucepan of salted boiling water for 7 minutes. Add the beans and cook for a further 5 minutes.

- To make the pesto, pound together all the ingredients in a mortar with a pestle to form a chunky pesto and season. Alternatively, place the ingredients in a small food processor or blender and whizz together.

- Drain the pasta and vegetables and return to a pan. Toss together with the pesto and season.

- Spoon into serving bowls and serve scattered with extra Parmesan and toasted pine nuts.

---

1 **Quick Bean and Pea Pasta with Red Pesto** Cook 500 g (1 lb) fresh trofie according to the pack instructions until al dente. Meanwhile, cook 75 g (3 oz) frozen broad beans, 75 g (3 oz) frozen peas and 125 g (4 oz) trimmed green beans in a separate saucepan of salted boiling water for 3–4 minutes or until tender. Drain the pasta and vegetables and return to a pan. Stir through 4 tablespoons shop-bought fresh red pesto and serve immediately.

3 **Roast Chicken with Potato, Green Bean and Pesto Pasta** Place the potatoes, prepared as above, in a roasting tin and toss in a little olive oil. Place in a preheated oven, 200°C (400°C), Gas Mark 6, for 5 minutes. Add 4 boneless chicken breasts to the tin and return to the oven for 20 minutes or until the potatoes and chicken are golden and cooked through. Meanwhile, cook the trofie as above. Add the green beans to the pan 5 minutes before the end of the cooking time and cook until tender. Make the pesto as above and mix together with 50 g (2 oz) soft goats' cheese in a bowl. Drain the pasta and beans and return to the pan. Stir through the pesto and roasted potatoes and serve the pasta alongside the chicken.

Chicken, Bacon and Asparagus, Pasta Bake

Serves 4

2 teaspoons olive oil
2 boneless, skinless chicken
   breasts
4 back bacon rashers
325 g (11 oz) penne
150 g (5 oz) asparagus spears,
   trimmed and thickly sliced
150 g (5 oz) crème fraîche
100 ml (3½ fl oz) milk
25 g (1 oz) Parmesan cheese,
   grated
salt and pepper

- Rub the oil over the chicken breasts and season well, then cook under a preheated hot grill for 7 minutes on each side or until golden and cooked through. Add the bacon to the grill pan when you turn over the chicken and cook until just crisp. Cool slightly, then chop into bite-sized pieces.

- Meanwhile, cook the pasta in a large saucepan of salted boiling water according to the pack instructions until al dente. Add the asparagus 3 minutes before the end of the cooking time and cook until just tender. Drain well and return to the pan.

- Mix together the crème fraîche and milk in a bowl, then stir into the pasta. Add the chicken and bacon and season well.

- Spoon into a large heatproof dish and scatter the Parmesan on top. Cook under a preheated hot grill for 5 minutes or until golden and heated through.

Asparagus and Chicken Penne with Parma Ham Cook the penne as above. Meanwhile, drizzle a little olive oil and balsamic vinegar over 150 g (5 oz) trimmed asparagus spears. Season, then cook on a hot griddle for 5 minutes, turning frequently, until soft. Chop into pieces. Drain the pasta, reserving a little of the cooking water, and return to the pan. Toss through the asparagus, 1 shop-bought roasted chicken breast, skin discarded and torn into strips, and 3 tablespoons crème fraîche. Serve topped with a slice of Parma ham.

Penne with Poached Chicken and Asparagus Place 2 boneless, skinless chicken breasts in a saucepan, pour over enough hot chicken stock to cover and add a good squeeze of lemon juice. Cook over a very gentle heat for 12–15 minutes or until cooked through. Remove from the pan, cut into bite-sized pieces and keep warm. Boil the poaching liquid for 5–10 minutes until reduced, then add 3 tablespoons crème fraîche and a few finely chopped tarragon leaves. Meanwhile, cook and drain the asparagus and penne as above. Toss through the creamy sauce and chicken. Serve immediately.

Creamy Anchovy, Lemon and Rocket Spaghetti

Serves 4

75 g (3 oz) ciabatta bread
1 tablespoon olive oil
1 garlic clove, crushed
400 g (13 oz) spaghetti
50 g (2 oz) rocket leaves
salt and pepper

For the anchovy sauce

8 anchovy fillets in oil, drained
3 tablespoons mascarpone
   cheese
juice of ½ lemon
1 egg, lightly beaten
25 g (1 oz) Parmesan cheese,
   grated

- Place the ciabatta in a food processor or blender and whizz to form chunky breadcrumbs. Heat the oil in a small frying pan, add the garlic and stir around the pan, then add the breadcrumbs. Cook for 5–7 minutes until golden and crisp all over, then remove from the pan and set aside.

- To make the anchovy sauce, mash the anchovies on a board, using the back of a large knife, to form a paste. Place in a bowl and mix in the mascarpone, then stir in the lemon juice, egg and Parmesan.

- Cook the pasta in a large saucepan of salted boiling water according to the pack instructions until al dente. Drain, reserving a little of the cooking water, and return to the pan. Stir in the anchovy sauce and mix together well, adding a little cooking water to loosen if needed. Season, then toss through the rocket leaves.

- Spoon into serving bowls and serve scattered with the breadcrumbs.

1 **Spaghetti with Buttery Anchovy, Lemon and Rocket Sauce**

Cook and drain the spaghetti as above. Meanwhile, place 8 drained anchovy fillets in oil, 50 g (2 oz) softened butter, the grated rind of 1 lemon and 75 g (3 oz) rocket leaves in a food processor or blender and whizz together. Stir the butter through the drained pasta and serve immediately.

3 **Caramelized Onion, Cavalo Nero and Anchovy Spaghetti**

Heat a little butter and olive oil in a frying pan, add 1 sliced onion and cook over a very low heat for 20–25 minutes until caramelized. Meanwhile, heat a little olive oil in a saucepan, add 1 sliced garlic clove and cook over a low heat until softened. Add 150 g (5 oz) cavalo nero and cook for 1–2 minutes, then pour over 100 ml (3½ fl oz) hot chicken stock and cook for a further 5 –7 minutes until tender. Make the anchovy sauce and cook and drain the spaghetti as above. Stir the caramelized onion, anchovy sauce and cavalo nero and any juices through the drained pasta. Serve immediately.

Chorizo and Red Pepper Pasta

Serves 2

200 g (7 oz) fiorelli pasta

1 tablespoon olive oil, plus extra to serve

75 g (3 fl oz) chorizo, thinly sliced

1 red pepper, cored, deseeded and cut into chunks

1 garlic clove, crushed

1 tablespoon tomato purée

75 ml (3 fl oz) dry white wine

teaspoon sugar

salt and pepper

chopped flat-leaf parsley, to garnish

- Cook the pasta in a large saucepan of salted boiling water according to the pack instructions until al dente.

- Meanwhile, heat the oil in a large frying pan, add the chorizo slices and cook, for a couple of seconds until crisp. Remove with a slotted spoon and set aside.

- Add the red pepper to the pan and cook for a couple of minutes until browned. Stir in the garlic and tomato purée and cook for a further 30 seconds. Pour over the wine, add the sugar and stir well. Bring to the boil, then cook for 5 minutes until reduced slightly and season.

- Drain the pasta and return to the pan. Toss with a little olive oil, then stir through the chorizo and sauce. Spoon into serving bowls and serve sprinkled with the parsley.

2 Paella-Style Red Pepper Pasta

Cook 1 boneless chicken breast under a preheated hot grill for 7 minutes on each side or until cooked through. Meanwhile, heat the olive oil in a large saucepan and fry 100 g (3½ oz) chorizo, cubed, and 1 red pepper, prepared as above, until browned, then add the wine as above, a pinch of saffron threads and 500 g (1 lb) cleaned clams. Cover with a lid and cook for 5 minutes, shaking occasionally, until the clams open. Discard any that remain closed. Cook 200 g (7 oz) orzo according to the pack instructions. Drain, then toss through the clam sauce and sliced chicken.

3 Pasta with Rich Red Pepper Sauce

Place the red pepper, prepared as above, and 3 halved tomatoes in a roasting tin and drizzle with a little olive oil and a splash of white wine. Place in a preheated oven, 190°C (375°F), Gas Mark 5, for 20–25 minutes. Meanwhile, cook and drain the fiorelli as above. Sprinkle the pepper and tomatoes with 1 teaspoon smoked paprika, then toss through the drained pasta. Serve with dollops of soured cream.

Linguine with Seafood in a Tomato Sauce

Serves 2

3 tablespoons olive oil
2 garlic cloves, sliced
1 red chilli, deseeded if liked, and finely chopped
75 ml (3 fl oz) dry white wine
250 g (8 oz) tomatoes, deseeded and chopped
500 g (1 lb) mussels, debearded and cleaned
200 g (7 oz) linguine
handful of flat-leaf parsley, chopped
salt and pepper

- Heat the oil in a large saucepan, add the garlic and chilli and cook for a couple of seconds until beginning to colour. Pour in the wine and cook for a couple of minutes until reduced by half. Stir in the tomatoes and cook for a further 5 minutes, adding a little water if needed.

- Add the mussels to the pan, cover with a lid and cook for 5 minutes, shaking occasionally, until the mussels open. Discard any that remain closed.

- Meanwhile, cook the pasta in a large saucepan of salted boiling water according to the pack instructions until al dente. Drain, toss through the mussel sauce and season. Scatter over the parsley and serve immediately.

Quick Seafood Linguine Cook the linguine as above. Meanwhile, heat 2 tablespoons olive oil in a frying pan, add 6 large scallops and cook for 2 minutes on each side or until just cooked through. Drain the pasta and return to the pan. Stir through the scallops, a good squeeze of lemon juice, 2 deseeded and chopped tomatoes and a pinch of dried chilli flakes. Serve immediately.

Cajun-Style Seafood Linguine Heat a little olive oil in a frying pan, add 150 g (5 oz) sliced smoked sausage and fry until golden. Add 1 chopped onion and cook until softened. Stir in 2 crushed garlic cloves and 1 teaspoon Cajun seasoning. Pour over a 400 g (13 oz) can chopped tomatoes and simmer for 20 minutes. Add the mussels, prepared as above, and continue as above.

Spaghetti Salsa Verde with Grilled Chicken

Serves 4

1 tablespoon olive oil
2 boneless, skinless chicken breasts
400 g (13 oz) spaghetti
salt and pepper

For the salsa verde

large handful of flat-leaf parsley
small handful of basil leaves
1 garlic clove, crushed
5 tablespoons extra-virgin olive oil
grated rind of 1 lemon, plus a squeeze of lemon juice
1–2 tablespoons capers, rinsed and drained

- Rub the 1 tablespoon oil over the chicken breasts and season well. Cook under a preheated hot grill for 7 minutes on each side or until golden and cooked through.

- Meanwhile, cook the pasta in a large saucepan of salted boiling water according to the pack instructions until al dente.

- To make the salsa verde, place the herbs, garlic, oil, lemon rind and lemon juice in a small food processor or blender. Pulse for a couple of seconds, then add the capers and pulse a few more times to form a thick paste.

- Drain the pasta, reserving a little of the cooking water, and return to the pan. Stir through the salsa verde, adding a little cooking water to loosen if needed, and season.

- Cut the chicken into thick slices. Spoon the pasta on to serving plates and serve topped with the sliced chicken.

---

1 **Simple Chicken and Salsa Verde Pasta Salad** Cook 500 g (1 lb) fresh penne according to the pack instructions until al dente. Meanwhile, make the salsa verde as above. Drain the pasta, then cool under cold running water and drain again. Tip into a serving dish and stir through the salsa verde. Add 2 shop-bought roasted chicken breasts, skin discarded and flesh torn into shreds, and 3 drained and chopped sun-dried tomatoes in oil.

3 **Chicken Pasta Soup with Salsa Verde** Place 1 sliced peeled carrot, 3 boneless, skinless chicken thighs and 1.5 litres (2½ pints) hot chicken stock in a large saucepan and gently poach for 20 minutes or until the chicken is cooked through. Remove the chicken with a slotted spoon and cool slightly, then cut into small strips. Return to the pan with a large handful of chopped Savoy cabbage and cook for 5 minutes until cooked through. Meanwhile, cook 100 g (3½ oz) orzo according to the pack instructions. Make the salsa verde as above. Drain the pasta, add to the soup and heat through. Serve with the salsa verde sauce drizzled over.

1 Broad Bean, Tomato and Goats' Cheese Pasta

Serves 2

200 g (7 oz) tricolore
   trottole pasta
75 g (3 oz) frozen broad beans,
   skinned if liked
1 tablespoon olive oil
1 garlic clove, sliced
125 g (4 oz) cherry tomatoes
50 g (2 oz) soft goats' cheese
salt and pepper
oregano leaves, to garnish

- Cook the pasta in a large saucepan of salted boiling water according to the pack instructions until al dente. Add the broad beans 3–4 minutes before the end of the cooking time and cook until tender.

- Meanwhile, heat the oil in a large frying pan, add the garlic and cook for 30 seconds, then stir in the tomatoes. Cook for a couple of minutes until soft, then squash with the back of a spoon to make a very rough sauce. Season well.

- Drain the pasta, reserving a little of the cooking water, and return to the pan. Toss through the tomato sauce, adding a little cooking water to loosen if needed.

- Spoon into serving bowls and crumble over the goats' cheese. Serve sprinkled with the oregano leaves.

2 Broad Bean, Tomato and Pancetta Pasta with Goats' Cheese

Heat a little olive oil in a large frying pan, add 5 slices of pancetta, cut into thin strips, and cook until turning golden. Add 1 sliced garlic clove and 50 ml (2 fl oz) dry white wine and cook until reduced, then add 200 g (7 oz) chopped tomatoes. Cook for 10 minutes, adding a little water. Meanwhile, cook the tricolore trottole and broad beans as above. Drain and stir through the sauce with a handful of chopped oregano leaves. Serve with the goats' cheese as above.

3 Tomato and Goats' Cheese Open Lasagne with Broad Bean Salad

Make the tomato sauce as above, adding 5 drained and chopped sun-dried tomatoes in oil with the cherry tomatoes. Pour over 100 ml (3½ fl oz) hot chicken stock and simmer for 10 minutes. Meanwhile, cook 4 dried lasagne sheets in a large saucepan of salted boiling water for 7–10 minutes or until soft, then drain well. Cut the sheets in half and lay one half-sheet on each of 4 plates. Divide half the sauce and 75 g (3 oz) crumbled soft goats' cheese over the pasta, then repeat the layers, finishing with goats' cheese. Toss 75 g (3 oz) cooked and skinned broad beans with a little chopped shallot, 50 g (2 oz) baby salad leaves, a squeeze of lemon juice and 2 tablespoons extra-virgin olive oil in a bowl. Arrange around each plate and serve immediately.

Mexican Chicken Tagliatelle

Serves 4

3 tablespoons olive oil
1 onion, finely chopped
2 garlic cloves, finely chopped
1 tablespoon tomato purée
400 g (13 oz) can chopped
  tomatoes
1 teaspoon chipotle paste or
  chipotle sauce
2 boneless, skinless chicken
  breasts
400 g (13 oz) tagliatelle
50 ml (2 fl oz) soured cream
salt and pepper
chopped coriander leaves,
  to garnish

· Heat 2 tablespoons of the oil in a saucepan, add the onion and cook for 3 minutes, stirring often. Add the garlic and cook for 2–3 minutes or until softened. Stir in the tomato purée, tomatoes and chipotle paste or sauce. Simmer for 20 minutes, adding a little water if needed, then season.

· Meanwhile, rub the remaining oil over the chicken breasts and season well. Heat a griddle pan until smoking, add the chicken and cook for 7 minutes on each side or until lightly charred and cooked through. Alternatively, cook under a preheated hot grill.

· Cook the pasta in a large saucepan of salted boiling water according to the pack instructions until al dente. Drain, reserving a little cooking water. Stir through the tomato sauce, adding a little cooking water to loosen if needed.

· Cut the chicken into bite-sized pieces and stir through the pasta. Spoon into serving bowls, sprinkle with the coriander and serve with dollops of soured cream.

Fiery Chicken Pasta Salad Cook 500 g (1 lb) fresh penne according to the pack instructions until al dente. Drain, then cool under cold running water and drain again. Meanwhile, chop 5 deseeded tomatoes, 2 spring onions, ½ red chilli, deseeded if liked, and mix in a bowl with a squeeze of lime juice and a drizzle of extra-virgin olive oil. Tip the pasta in a serving dish and mix well with the tomato mixture and 1 shop-bought roasted chicken breast, skin discarded and flesh shredded.

Tagliatelle with Chicken and Spicy Tomato Sauce Place 2 boneless, skinless chicken breasts in a small pan, pour over enough chicken stock to cover and cook over a very gentle heat for 10–15 minutes or until cooked through. Meanwhile, place 250 g (8 oz) cherry tomatoes and 1 chopped red chilli, deseeded if liked, in a grill pan and toss in a little olive oil. Cook under a preheated hot grill for 10 minutes or until blackened. Peel away the skin, seeds and membrane. Place in a small food processor or blender with 5 tablespoons soured cream and a handful of coriander leaves and whizz together. While the chicken and tomatoes are cooking, cook the tagliatelle as above. Drain, reserving a little of the cooking water, and return to the pan. Stir through the tomato sauce, adding a little cooking water to loosen if needed. Cut the chicken into slices and mix in. Serve sprinkled with extra chopped coriander, if liked.

Lemony Conchiglie with Tuna and Capers

Serves 4

400 g (13 oz) conchiglie
1 small garlic clove, crushed
juice and grated rind of ½ lemon
5 tablespoons extra-virgin
  olive oil
225 g (7½ oz) can tuna in oil,
  drained
2 tablespoons capers, rinsed and
  drained
large handful of flat-leaf parsley,
  chopped
salt and pepper

• Cook the pasta in a large saucepan of salted boiling water according to the pack instructions until al dente.

• Meanwhile, mix together the garlic, lemon juice and rind and olive oil in a bowl. Using a fork, break the tuna into large chunks and carefully stir into the dressing with the capers.

• Drain the pasta, reserving a little of the cooking water, and return to the pan. Stir through the tuna and dressing, adding a little cooking water to loosen if needed. Season well, then stir in the parsley and serve immediately.

Quick Tuna, Caper and Lemon Pasta

Cook 200 g (7 oz) orzo according to the pack instructions. Meanwhile, whisk together 2 tablespoons extra-virgin olive oil and a squeeze of lemon juice, then stir in the tuna and capers as above. Drain the pasta and return to the pan. Stir through the tuna dressing, then toss through 75 g (3 oz) chopped rocket leaves. Serve immediately.

Fresh Tuna, Caper and Lemon

Conchiglie Season 2 thick tuna steaks, rub all over with olive oil and place in an ovenproof dish. Place in a preheated oven, 110°C (225°F), Gas Mark ¼, for 20–25 minutes, depending how rare you like it. Meanwhile, cook and drain the conchiglie above. Cut the fish into large chunks and toss through the pasta with a little chopped red onion, 2 tablespoons rinsed and drained capers, a squeeze of lemon juice and a handful of chopped flat-leaf parsley. Serve immediately.

Creamy Broccoli and Anchovy Orecchiette

Serves 4

2 tablespoons olive oil
15 g (½ oz) butter
1 onion, sliced
3 garlic cloves, sliced
½ teaspoon dried chilli flakes
8 anchovy fillets in oil, drained
100 ml (3½ fl oz) double cream
125 g (4 oz) tenderstem broccoli
400 g (13 oz) orecchiette pasta
salt and pepper

- Heat the oil and butter in a large frying pan, add the onion and cook for 10 minutes until soft and golden. Add the garlic, chilli flakes and anchovies and cook for a further 2–3 minutes or until the anchovies begin to disintegrate. Mash them with the back of a spoon, pour over the cream and season.

- Meanwhile, cook the broccoli in a large saucepan of salted boiling water for 3 minutes, then remove with a slotted spoon. Add the pasta to the pan of boiling water and cook according to the pack instructions until al dente.

- Stir the broccoli into the anchovy sauce, cover with a lid and cook for 3–5 minutes or until the broccoli is cooked through.

- Drain the pasta, reserving a little of the cooking water, and stir through the broccoli sauce, adding a little cooking water to loosen if needed. Serve immediately.

Orecchiette with Chunky Broccoli Sauce Cook 500 g (1 lb) fresh orecchiette according to the pack instructions until al dente. Meanwhile, cook 150 g (5 oz) purple sprouting broccoli spears in a saucepan of boiling water for 5 minutes until tender. Drain the broccoli and place in a food processor or blender with 1 crushed garlic clove, 3 drained and mashed anchovy fillets in oil, the grated rind and juice of ½ lemon, 25 g (1 oz) grated Parmesan cheese, a pinch of dried chilli flakes and 4 table-spoons extra-virgin olive oil and whizz together to form a chunky sauce. Drain the pasta, reserving a little of the cooking water, and return to the pan. Toss through the broccoli sauce, adding a little cooking water to loosen if needed, and serve immediately.

Anchovy Orecchiette with Roasted Broccoli Toss 1 head of broccoli, cut into florets, in 3 tablespoons olive oil and season. Place in an ovenproof dish and bake in a preheated oven, 200°C (400°F), Gas Mark 6, for 20–25 minutes until tender and lightly charred. Meanwhile, cook and drain the orecchiette as above. Mash the anchovies as above and 1 garlic clove together in a bowl. Stir through the paste, adding a little cooking water to loosen. Add the roasted broccoli and serve with grated Parmesan cheese.

Chicken Fusilli with Red Pepper and Almond Pesto

Serves 4

400 g (13 oz) fusilli
2 shop-bought roasted chicken
    breasts, about 150 g (5 oz) each
salt

For the pesto

5 tablespoons extra-virgin
    olive oil
2 red peppers
large handful of basil leaves,
    plus extra to garnish
25 g (1 oz) toasted almonds
25 g (1 oz) Pecorino cheese,
    grated, plus extra to serve

- To make the pesto, rub about 1 tablespoon of the olive oil over the red peppers. Cook under a preheated hot grill for 10 minutes, turning, until charred all over. Place in a plastic food bag, seal and leave for 5 minutes. When cooled, peel off the blackened skin. Cut in half and remove the seeds.

- Place the roasted peppers in a food processor or blender with the remaining olive oil, basil, almonds and Pecorino and whizz to form a thick but smooth paste. Add a little more oil or a drizzle of water if needed. Season well with salt.

- Meanwhile, cook the pasta in a large saucepan of salted boiling water according to the packet instructions until al dente. Drain, reserving a little of the cooking water, and return to the pan. Stir in the pesto, adding a little cooking water to loosen until the pasta is coated.

- Tear the chicken into strips, discarding the skin, and stir through the pasta. Serve in bowls sprinkled with a little extra chopped basil and grated Pecorino.

---

1 Easy Red Pepper and Almond Pasta Salad Cook the fusilli as above. Drain, then cool under cold running water and drain again. Meanwhile, place 25 g (1 oz) each toasted almonds and Pecorino cheese and 4 table-spoons mayonnaise in a small food processor or blender and whizz together. Tip the pasta into a large dish and toss through the sauce, 2 drained and chopped roasted red peppers from a jar and a handful of chopped basil leaves. Sprinkle with 25 g (1 oz) flaked almonds.

3 Grilled Chicken with Spicy Red Pepper and Almond Fusilli Rub a little olive oil over 1 red chilli and grill alongside the red peppers as above, then make the red pepper and almond pesto as above, adding the peeled and deseeded chilli. Mix together 75 g (3 oz) soft goats' cheese with a handful of chopped basil leaves in a bowl. Spread a little of the mixture under the skin of 4 boneless chicken breasts, then cook under a preheated hot grill for about 7 minutes on each side or until cooked through.

Meanwhile, cook and drain 300 g (10 oz) fusilli as above. Stir through the pesto, adding a little cooking water to loosen, and serve alongside the chicken with extra toasted almonds scattered over.

Creamy Gorgonzola Gnocchi

Serves 4

25 g (1 oz) butter
2 leeks, trimmed, cleaned
   and sliced
1 onion, sliced
1 garlic clove, finely chopped
75 ml (3 fl oz) double cream
75 g (3 oz) Gorgonzola cheese
500 g (1 lb) pack fresh gnocchi
25 g (1 oz) toasted walnuts,
   roughly chopped
salt and pepper

- Heat the butter in a saucepan, add the leeks and onion and a splash of water and cook over a low heat for 15 minutes until very soft. Stir in the garlic and cook for a further 1 minute. Add the cream and crumble over the Gorgonzola, then cook until the cheese melts.

- Meanwhile, cook the pasta in a large saucepan of salted boiling water according to the pack instructions. Drain, reserving a little of the cooking water, and return to the pan. Stir through the sauce, adding a little cooking water to loosen if needed. Season well.

- Spoon into serving bowls and serve topped with the walnuts.

Quick Gorgonzola and Spinach Gnocchi
Cook and drain the gnocchi as above, adding 250 g (8 oz) baby spinach leaves to the pan before draining. Stir through 75 g (3 oz) crumbled Gorgonzola cheese and enough cooking water to make a sauce. Serve at once.

Gnocchi with Roasted Shallots and Gorgonzola Toss 150 g (5 oz) shallots in 3 tablespoons olive oil and 1 tablespoon balsamic vinegar in a roasting tin, then scatter with a few thyme sprigs. Place in a preheated oven, 180°C (350°F), Gas Mark 4, for 20–25 minutes until soft and golden. Cook and drain the gnocchi as above. Stir through the roasted shallots, adding a little cooking water to loosen. Serve scattered with 75 g (3 oz) crumbled Gorgonzola cheese.

Linguine with Chicory, Pancetta and Mascarpone

Serves 2

1 tablespoon olive oil
50 g (2 oz) cubed pancetta
1 small onion, sliced
1 garlic clove, sliced
2 red chicory, trimmed and
thinly sliced
50 ml (2 fl oz) dry white wine
50 ml (2 fl oz) hot chicken stock
200 g (7 oz) linguine
25 g (1 oz) mascarpone cheese
15 g (½ oz) Parmesan cheese,
grated, plus extra to serve
salt and pepper

· Heat the oil in a frying pan, add the pancetta and cook until it begins to colour. Add the onion and cook for 5 minutes or until it begins to soften and turn golden.

· Add the garlic and cook for 30 seconds, then stir in the chicory. Cook for a few minutes until it wilts, then pour over the wine. Cook until reduced by half, then pour over the stock and simmer for 7 minutes.

· Meanwhile, cook the pasta in a large saucepan of salted boiling water according to the pack instructions until al dente. Drain, reserving a little of the cooking water and return to the pan.

· Stir the mascarpone and Parmesan into the sauce, season well and toss through the pasta, adding a little cooking water to loosen if needed. Spoon on to serving plates and serve scattered with extra Parmesan.

1 Linguine with Grilled Chicory, Pancetta and Mascarpone
Cook the linguine as above. Toss 2 heads of quartered chicory in a little olive oil. Place on a grill rack and cook under a hot grill for 2 minutes on each side, then drizzle with 2 teaspoons balsamic vinegar. Heat a little olive oil in a frying pan, add 75 g (3 oz) pancetta cubes and fry for 5 minutes until golden. Drain the pasta. Return to the pan. Toss through the chicory and pancetta. Serve with dollops of mascarpone and grated Parmesan cheese.

3 Roasted Chicory, Pancetta and Mascarpone Linguine Halve 4 heads of chicory and place in a roasting tin. Dab with a little butter and then pour over 100 ml (3½ fl oz) chicken stock. Place in a preheated oven, 180°C (350°F), Gas Mark 4, for 20–25 minutes or until golden and soft. Meanwhile, cook and drain the linguine and fry the pancetta, onion and garlic as above. Cut the roasted chicory into thin wedges and stir through the pasta with the pancetta mixture, mascarpone and Parmesan as above.

Prawn, Tomato and Feta Rigatoni

Serves 4

2 tablespoons olive oil
1 onion, finely chopped
2 garlic cloves, finely chopped
1 teaspoon tomato purée
juice of ½ lemon
1 teaspoon sugar
½ teaspoon dried chilli flakes
400 g (13 oz) can chopped
    tomatoes
200 g (7 oz) frozen large raw
    peeled prawns
400 g (13 oz) rigatoni
50 g (2 oz) feta cheese
salt and pepper
chopped flat-leaf parsley,
    to garnish

· Heat the oil in a saucepan, add the onion and garlic and cook for a couple of minutes until softened. Stir in the tomato purée, then add the lemon juice, sugar, chilli flakes and tomatoes. Bring to the boil, then reduce the heat and simmer for 10 minutes.

· Remove the pan from the heat then, using a stick blender, whizz to a smooth purée. Return to the heat, add the prawns and cook for 3–5 minutes or until they have turned pink and are just cooked through and season well.

· Meanwhile, cook the pasta in a large saucepan of salted boiling water according to the pack instructions until al dente. Drain, reserving a little of the cooking water, and return to the pan. Stir through the prawn sauce, adding a little cooking water if needed. Spoon into serving bowls, then crumble over the feta and serve sprinkled with the parsley.

---

10 Prawn Penne with No-Cook Tomato Sauce and Feta Cook 500 g (1 lb) fresh penne according to pack instructions until al dente. Add the prawns to the pan 5 minutes before the end of the cooking time and cook until they are pink and are cooked through. Meanwhile, mix 2 chopped and deseeded tomatoes, 1 table-spoon sweet chilli sauce and a handful of chopped basil leaves in a bowl. Drain the pasta and prawns and return to the pan. Drizzle with olive oil, mix in the tomato sauce and serve with 50 g (2 oz) feta cheese.

30 One-Pot Tomato, Prawn and Feta Rigatoni Heat 500 g (1 lb) shop-bought tomato sauce with 200 ml (7 fl oz) fish stock. Simmer for 10 minutes, as above, then stir 400 g (14 oz) rigatoni into the pan and cook for a further 10 minutes, stirring occasionally. Stir through the prawns as above and cook for 3–5 minutes or until they have turned pink and are just cooked through. Mix together 50 g (2 oz) crumbled feta cheese, a handful of fresh white breadcrumbs and a handful of chopped flat-leaf parsley and scatter over. Cook under a preheated hot grill for a couple of minutes until golden.

Bucatini with Sardines and Fennel

Serves 4

pinch of saffron threads
5 tablespoons boiling water
3 tablespoons olive oil
1 garlic clove, finely chopped
50 g (2 oz) fresh white
   breadcrumbs
400 g (13 oz) bucatini pasta
1 onion, chopped
1 fennel bulb, chopped
1 teaspoon fennel seeds
2 anchovy fillets in oil, drained
2 tablespoons raisins
4 sardines, boned and filleted
2 tablespoons toasted pine nuts
handful of dill, chopped
salt and pepper

- Place the saffron in a small bowl and pour over the measurement water. Leave to stand for 5 minutes. Meanwhile, heat 1 tablespoon of the oil in a small frying pan, add the garlic and breadcrumbs and cook for a couple of minutes until golden. Set aside.

- Cook the pasta in a large saucepan of salted boiling water according to the pack instructions until al dente. Meanwhile, heat another tablespoon of the oil in a large frying pan, add the onion and both kinds of fennel and cook for 5 minutes to soften. Mash in the anchovies, then add the saffron with its soaking water. Add the raisins and let it bubble for 2 minutes.

- Rub the remaining tablespoon of oil over the sardine fillets and season well. Cook on a preheated hot griddle pan or under a hot grill for 3 minutes on each side or until cooked through. Drain the pasta, reserving a little of the cooking water, and return to the pan. Toss through the sauce, adding a little cooking water to loosen if needed. Season well. Spoon on to serving plates, top with the sardine fillets. Serve scattered with the pine nuts, breadcrumbs and dill.

 Quick Sardine Spaghettini
Cook 400 g (13 oz) spaghettini according to the pack instructions until al dente. Meanwhile, place a 120 g (4 oz) can sardines in tomato sauce and 1 chopped tomato in a small saucepan and heat through. Stir in 1 tablespoon rinsed and drained capers. Drain the pasta, reserving some cooking water, and return to the pan. Stir through the sauce, adding a little cooking water to loosen, and serve immediately.

 Sardine and Tomato Bucatini with Walnut Pesto Heat a little olive oil in a saucepan, add 1 chopped tomato and gently cook until softened. Add 1 chopped garlic clove and a splash of balsamic vinegar, then pour over 300 ml (½ pint) passata and cook for 10 minutes. Add a drained 120 g (4 oz) can sardines in oil and cook for a further 10 minutes. Meanwhile, cook and drain the bucatini as above. Place 75 g (3 oz) walnuts, 1 garlic clove, a squeeze of lemon juice, 1 tablespoon rinsed and drained capers, 5 tablespoons extra-virgin olive oil and a handful of basil leaves in a food processor or blender and whizz together to form a pesto. Stir the sardine sauce through the drained pasta and serve with the walnut pesto drizzled over.

Tortelloni with Easy Olive and Tomato Sauce

Serves 4

2 tablespoons olive oil

1 garlic clove, sliced

75 g (3 oz) pitted black olives

150 g (5 oz) cherry tomatoes, halved

handful of basil leaves

500 g (1 lb) pack cheese tortelloni

salt and pepper

- Heat a medium-sized frying pan until hot, then add the oil. Add the garlic and olives and cook for 30 seconds until beginning to sizzle, then tip in the tomatoes and cook for a couple of minutes or until the tomatoes are beginning to soften. Season and stir in the basil leaves.

- Meanwhile, cook the pasta in a large saucepan of salted boiling water according to the pack instructions. Drain and toss together with the tomato sauce. Serve immediately.

---

2 **Farfalle with Olive Tapenade and Tomato** Cook 400 g (13 oz) farfalle according to the pack instructions until al dente. Meanwhile, place 1 crushed garlic clove, the juice of ½ lemon, 3 drained anchovy fillets in oil, 100 g (3½ oz) pitted black olives, a handful of flat-leaf parsley and 3 tablespoons extra-virgin olive oil in a food processor or blender and whizz together to form a rough paste. Drain the pasta, reserving a little of the cooking water, and return to the pan. Stir through the tapenade, adding a little cooking water to loosen, and 2 chopped tomatoes. Serve immediately.

---

3 **Homemade Four-Cheese Pasta Pockets with Tomato and Olive Sauce** Mix together 100 g (3½ oz) cream cheese, 75 g (3 oz) dolcelatte cheese, 75 g (3 oz) grated Gruyère cheese and 25 g (1 oz) grated Parmesan cheese in a bowl. Lay 4 shop-bought fresh pasta sheets on a lightly floured work surface. Using a 4 in cutter, stamp out 16 rounds from the sheets. Alternatively, use 16 wonton or gyoza wrappers. Brush a little egg yolk around the edges of the rounds and place 1 teaspoon of the filling in the centre of each, then fold in half and use your fingers to seal.

Cook in batches in a large saucepan of salted boiling water for 3 minutes. Meanwhile, heat through 350 ml (12 fl oz) shop-bought tomato pasta sauce and 75 g (3 oz) pitted black olives in a saucepan. Drain the pasta and return to the pan, then toss through the tomato sauce. Serve immediately.

20 Spanish Seafood Pasta

Serves 4

2 tablespoons olive oil

1 onion, finely chopped

1 garlic clove, crushed

1 teaspoon tomato purée

1 teaspoon paprika

125 ml (4 fl oz) dry white wine

400 g (13 oz) can chopped tomatoes

1 litre (1¾ pints) hot chicken stock

300 g (10 oz) angel hair pasta

200 g (7 oz) mussels, debearded and cleaned

125 g (4 oz) large cooked unpeeled prawns

75 g (3 oz) prepared squid rings, cleaned

- Heat the oil in a large saucepan, add the onion and garlic and cook over a medium heat for 5 minutes or until softened. Stir in the tomato purée and paprika, then pour over the wine and bubble for 1–2 minutes until reduced a little. Pour in the tomatoes and stock and bring to the boil.

- Break the pasta into small lengths about 2.5 cm (1 inch) long. Reduce the heat so the mixture is simmering and stir the pasta into the pan. Cover with a lid and cook for 7 minutes, stirring occasionally to stop the pasta from sticking.

- Add the mussels, cover and cook for 3 minutes until the mussels begin to open. Add the squid rings and prawns and cook for a further 2 minutes or until the seafood is cooked through and all the mussels have opened. Discard any mussels that remain closed.

- Bring the pan to the table and serve.

---

10 Seafood Pasta Salad Cook 300 g (10 oz) orzo according to the pack instructions. Add 125 g (4 oz) cooked peeled prawns 3 minutes and 75 g (3 oz) squid rings 1 minute before the end of the cooking time and cook until the seafood is cooked through. Cool under cold water and drain again. Tip into a serving dish and toss with a squeeze of lemon juice, 2 tablespoons extra-virgin olive oil, 2 chopped tomatoes, 50 g (2 oz) rocket leaves and a handful of pitted black olives.

30 Spanish Seafood Pasta with Chicken Rub a little olive oil over 2 boneless chicken breasts and place in a roasting tin. Cook in a preheated oven, 200°C (400°F), Gas Mark 6, for 20 minutes or until cooked through. Meanwhile, make the recipe as above. Cut the chicken into slices, discarding the skin, and add to the pan with the squid for the last 2 minutes of cooking.

Sweet Potato and Spinach Penne

Serves 4

2 sweet potatoes, peeled and cut into bite-sized pieces

1 head of garlic, cloves separated

4 tablespoons olive oil

1 tablespoon white balsamic vinegar

400 g (13 oz) penne

200 g (7 oz) baby spinach leaves

50 g (2 oz) feta cheese

salt and pepper

- Place the sweet potato and garlic on a baking sheet. Drizzle over 2 tablespoons of the oil and toss until coated, then season. Place in a preheated oven, 180°C (350°F), Gas Mark 4, for 15–20 minutes until the sweet potato is soft and lightly charred.

- Squeeze the garlic out of its skin into a bowl and mash lightly with a fork to form a paste, then stir in the vinegar and remaining oil. Season well.

- Meanwhile, cook the pasta in a large saucepan of salted boiling water according to the pack instructions until al dente. Tip in the spinach, then drain and return to the pan.

- Stir the garlic sauce into the pasta with the roasted sweet potato. Spoon on to serving plates and serve with the feta cheese crumbled over.

Quick Sweet Potato and Spinach Penne

Cook the penne as above. Add 2 peeled sweet potatoes, cut into bite-sized pieces, to the pan 7 minutes before the end of the cooking time and cook until soft. Add 200 g (7 oz) baby spinach leaves, then drain and return to the pan. Toss together with 100 g (3½ oz) ricotta cheese mixed with 25 g (1 oz) grated Parmesan cheese. Serve immediately.

Penne with Spinach and Sweet Potato Sauce

Halve 2 sweet potatoes and place on a baking sheet. Roast in a preheated oven, 180°C (350°F), Gas Mark 4, for 25–30 minutes until softened. Scoop out the flesh with a fork and mash together with 75 g (3 oz) mascarpone cheese in a bowl. Meanwhile, cook the penne and spinach as above. Drain, reserving a little of the cooking water, and return to the pan. Toss through the sweet potato sauce, adding a little cooking water to loosen. Serve immediately.

 # Pasta with Pork and Mushrooms in a White Wine Sauce

Serves 4

2 tablespoons olive oil
1 onion, finely chopped
1 garlic clove, finely chopped
450 g (14½ oz) minced pork
1 tablespoon tomato purée
250 ml (8 fl oz) dry white wine
150 ml (¼ pint) hot chicken stock
150 g (5 oz) mushrooms, trimmed
   and chopped
75 ml (3 fl oz) double cream
400 g (13 oz) lumaconi pasta
25 g (1 oz) Parmesan cheese,
   grated, plus extra to serve
salt and pepper
chopped flat-leaf parsley, to
   garnish

- Heat 1 tablespoon of the oil in a large frying pan, add the onion and cook for a couple of minutes until beginning to soften. Add the garlic and pork and cook, breaking up the meat with the back of a spoon, for 5–10 minutes or until the meat is golden.

- Stir in the tomato purée and cook for a further 1 minute. Pour over the wine and cook until reduced by half, then add the chicken stock and simmer for 10 minutes.

- Heat the remaining oil in a separate frying pan. Add the mushrooms and cook for 3 minutes or until golden and soft. Add to the pork, then stir in the cream.

- Meanwhile, cook the pasta in a large saucepan of salted boiling water according to the pack instructions until al dente. Drain, reserving a little of the cooking water, and return to the pan. Stir through the sauce and Parmesan, adding a little cooking water to loosen if needed. Season well.

- Spoon into serving bowls and serve sprinkled with the parsley and extra Parmesan.

1 Mushroom and Parma Ham Pasta

Cook and drain 400 g (13 oz) penne. Meanwhile, fry the mushrooms as above, adding 1 chopped garlic clove. When golden, stir through the pasta with the grated rind and juice of 1 lemon and 6 slices of Parma ham, torn into strips. Toss through a handful of rocket leaves, if liked. Serve immediately.

2 Pasta with Spicy Pork and Mushrooms

Cook 4 thin pork chops under a preheated medium grill for 7 minutes on each side or until cooked through. Add the mushrooms to the grill pan 5 minutes before the end of the cooking time. Mix together the grated rind and juice of 1 lemon, 1 teaspoon fennel seeds, 1 chopped red chilli, deseeded if liked, and 5 tablespoons crème fraîche in a bowl. Meanwhile, cook and drain the lumaconi as above. Slice the pork into thin strips and toss through the pasta with the mushrooms, crème fraîche and 2 chopped tomatoes. Serve immediately.

QuickCook
Family Favourites

Recipes listed by cooking time

10

30 Cheesy Tomato Pasta Bake

Serves 4

2 tablespoons olive oil, plus extra
for greasing
2 garlic cloves, finely chopped
400 g (13 oz) can chopped
tomatoes
handful of oregano leaves,
chopped, plus extra to garnish
400 g (13 oz) penne
250 g (8 oz) mozzarella cheese,
cubed
50 g (2 oz) Parmesan cheese,
grated
salt and pepper

- Heat the oil in a large frying pan, add the garlic and cook for 30 seconds. Stir in the tomatoes and oregano and simmer, fairly vigorously, for 10–12 minutes or until thickened. Season well.

- Meanwhile, cook the pasta in a large saucepan of salted boiling water according to the pack instructions until al dente. Drain, reserving a little of the cooking water, and return to the pan. Stir in the tomato sauce, reserving 2 tablespoons of the sauce. Add a little cooking water to loosen if needed.

- Spoon half the pasta into a greased ovenproof dish. Cover with half the mozzarella and Parmesan, then add the remaining pasta. Spoon over the reserved tomato sauce and scatter with the remaining cheese.

- Place in a preheated oven, 200°C (400°F), Gas Mark 6, for 15 minutes or until golden and bubbling and serve.

10 Simple Cheese and Tomato Penne

Cook and drain the penne as above. Stir through 4 chopped tomatoes, 3 tablespoons crème fraîche and a handful of chopped rocket leaves. Served topped with 150 g (5 oz) sliced mozzarella cheese and a little grated Parmesan cheese.

20 Bubbling Tomato, Cheese and Ham

Penne Cook the penne as above. Meanwhile, place 500 ml (17 fl oz) shop-bought tomato pasta sauce and 200 g (7 oz) ham, cut into chunks, in a large saucepan and heat through. Drain the pasta and stir through the sauce. Spoon into a heatproof dish, then scatter over 150 g (5 oz) grated Gruyère cheese and cook under a preheated medium grill for 10 minutes or until golden and bubbling.

 # Spaghetti Carbonara

Serves 4

400 g (13 oz) spaghetti
150 g (5 oz) streaky bacon
2 egg yolks
4 tablespoons double cream
25 g (1 oz) Parmesan cheese,
   grated, plus extra to serve
salt and pepper
green salad, to serve

- Cook the pasta in a large saucepan of salted boiling water according to the pack instructions until al dente.

- Meanwhile, cook the bacon under a preheated medium grill for 7 minutes or until crisp. Cool for 1 minute, then cut into small pieces. Mix together the egg yolks, cream and Parmesan in a bowl.

- Drain the pasta, reserving a little of the cooking water, and return to the pan. Stir in the bacon and cream mixture, adding a little cooking water to loosen if needed. Season well.

- Pile on to serving plates, scatter with extra Parmesan and serve with a green salad.

2 **Summery Spaghetti Carbonara** Heat 1 tablespoon olive oil in a frying pan with 2 thickly sliced courgettes and cook for 8 minutes, turning once until the courgettes are golden. Add 1 sliced garlic clove and 2 sliced spring onions and cook for 30 seconds. Meanwhile, make the recipe as above, stirring the courgettes into the pasta with the bacon and cream mixture. Serve sprinkled with chopped basil leaves.

3 **Spaghetti Carbonara with Poached Eggs** Crack 1 egg into a small cup. Bring a shallow pan of water to the boil, stir the water vigorously to make a whirlpool, then gently slide the egg into the centre. Leave to cook for 3 minutes, then lift out with a slotted spoon, pat dry with kitchen paper and keep warm. Repeat with 3 more eggs. Meanwhile, make the recipe as above and serve topped with the eggs.

Classic Minestrone

Serves 4

2 tablespoons olive oil

1 onion, chopped

1 carrot, peeled and chopped

1 celery stick, chopped

1 teaspoon tomato purée

2 garlic cloves, finely chopped

400 g (13 oz) can chopped
tomatoes

750 ml (1¼ pints) hot chicken or
vegetable stock

2 thyme sprigs, leaves stripped

125 g (4 oz) ditalini pasta

400 g (13 oz) can cannellini beans,
rinsed and drained

½ head of Savoy cabbage,
shredded

salt and pepper

grated Parmesan cheese,
to serve

- Heat the oil in a large saucepan, add the onion, carrot and celery and cook over a low heat for 10 minutes until really soft.

- Stir in the tomato purée and garlic, then add the tomatoes, stock and thyme and simmer for 10 minutes.

- Add the pasta and beans to the soup and cook for a further 10 minutes or until the pasta is cooked through. Add the cabbage 5 minutes before the end of the cooking time and cook until tender. Season well.

- Ladle into serving bowls and serve scattered with the Parmesan.

---

1 Speedy Springtime Minestrone

Heat 1 tablespoon olive oil in a large saucepan, add 1 crushed garlic clove and cook for 30 seconds. Pour over 1 litre (1¾ pints) boiling vegetable stock, then stir in 125 g (4 oz) ditalini pasta and cook for 8 minutes or until cooked through. Add 50 g (2 oz) trimmed green beans and 1 large chopped and deseeded tomato 5 minutes before the end of the cooking time, and 50 g (2 oz) frozen broad beans and 50 g (2 oz) frozen peas 3–4 minutes before the end of the cooking time, cooking until the vegetables are tender. Serve as above.

2 Simple Ham and Bean Soup

Pour 350 ml (12 fl oz) shop-bought tomato pasta sauce and 1 litre (1¾ pints) hot chicken stock into a large saucepan and simmer for 5 minutes. Add 200 g (7 oz) cubed ham and a rinsed and drained 400 g (13 oz) can cannellini or borlotti beans, then simmer for a further 5 minutes. Add 125 g (4 oz) ditalini pasta and cook for 10 minutes or until the pasta is cooked through. Serve sprinkled with basil leaves.

Four-Cheese Pasta with Watercress Salad

Serves 4

400 g (13 oz) messicani pasta
200 g (7 oz) mascarpone cheese
  or cream cheese
75 g (3 oz) mild Gorgonzola
  cheese, crumbled
75 g (3 oz) Fontina cheese, grated
25 g (1 oz) Parmesan cheese,
  grated
salt and pepper

For the watercress salad

1 teaspoon white wine vinegar
1 tablespoon extra virgin olive oil
75 g (3 oz) watercress

- Cook the pasta in a large saucepan of salted boiling water according to the pack instructions until al dente. Drain, reserving at least 50 ml (2 fl oz) of the cooking water, and return to the pan. Stir in the cheeses, adding enough of the cooking water to make a creamy sauce, and season.

- Whisk together the vinegar and oil, then toss together with the watercress in a bowl and season well.

- Spoon the pasta into serving bowls and serve topped with the watercress salad.

---

1 **Four-Cheese Tortelloni with Yogurt and Watercress**
Tip 150 g (5 oz) natural yogurt into a heatproof bowl, place over a saucepan of simmering water (making sure the bottom of the bowl doesn't touch the water) and heat through for 5 minutes. Meanwhile, cook 500 g (1 lb) four-cheese tortelloni according to the pack instructions, then drain and return to the pan. Toss through the yogurt and a handful of chopped watercress. Serve immediately.

3 **Four-Cheese Penne and Watercress Bake** Cook 400 g (13 oz) penne according to the pack instructions until al dente. Meanwhile, cook 6 bacon rashers under a preheated medium grill for 10 minutes or until crisp. Cool for 1 minute, then cut into bite-sized pieces. Mix together the four cheeses as above with 100 ml (3½ fl oz) milk in a bowl. Drain the pasta and return to the pan. Stir through the bacon and cheese sauce, add 100 g (3½ oz)
chopped watercress, then place in a heatproof dish. Top with 50 g (2 oz) fresh white breadcrumbs and cook under a preheated medium grill for 15 minutes or until golden and bubbling.

No-Chop Tomato and Rocket Pasta Salad

Serves 4

325 g (11 oz) tricolore trofie
50 g (2 oz) mayonnaise
50 g (2 oz) fromage frais
25 g (1 oz) Parmesan cheese, grated
125 g (4 oz) sunblush tomatoes in oil, drained
75 g (3 oz) rocket leaves
salt and pepper

- Cook the pasta in a large saucepan of salted boiling water according to the pack instructions until al dente. Drain, then cool under cold running water and drain again.

- Meanwhile, mix together the mayonnaise, fromage frais and Parmesan in a large serving bowl and season. Stir the tomatoes and rocket through the pasta and serve the mayonnaise alongside the pasta.

Tomato and Rocket Orzo Cook and drain 325 g (11 oz) orzo according to the pack instructions. Meanwhile, place 125 g (4 oz) drained sunblush tomatoes in oil and 50 g (2 oz) fromage frais in a food processor or blender and whizz to form a sauce. Toss through the drained pasta with 75 g (3 oz) rocket leaves. Serve immediately.

Aubergine, Tomato and Rocket Warm Pasta Salad Cut 1 aubergine into cubes and place in an ovenproof dish. Toss with plenty of olive oil and scatter with salt and a little dried chilli. Cook in a preheated oven, 180°C (350°F), Gas Mark 4, for 20–25 minutes or until soft. Leave to cool slightly. Meanwhile, cook the pasta as above. Drain and cool a little, then tip into a serving dish. Toss with 1 tablespoon balsamic vinegar, the sunblush tomatoes as above, the aubergine and 2 tablespoons extra virgin olive oil. Toss through the rocket to serve.

 # Pea Fusilli with Bacon and Ricotta

Serves 4

5 tablespoons olive oil

2 garlic cloves

175 g (6 oz) frozen peas

handful of mint leaves, chopped, plus extra to garnish (optional)

squeeze of lemon juice, plus grated lemon rind to garnish

400 g (13 oz) fusilli

4 streaky bacon rashers

25 g (1 oz) Parmesan cheese, grated, plus extra to serve

100 g (3½ oz) ricotta cheese, crumbled

salt and pepper

- Heat the oil in a small frying pan, add the garlic and cook over a very low heat for 5 minutes or until soft and golden.

- Cook the peas in a small saucepan of boiling water for 2–3 minutes or until just tender. Drain, then cool under cold running water and drain again. Place half the peas, the garlicky oil, reserving a little to coat the pasta, the garlic cloves, mint, lemon juice to taste and salt and pepper in a food processor or blender and whizz together.

- Cook the pasta in a large saucepan of salted boiling water according to the pack instructions until al dente. Cook the bacon under a preheated medium grill for 10 minutes, turning once, or until crisp and cooked through.

- Drain the pasta, reserving a little of the cooking water, and return to the pan. Toss through the reserved garlicky oil, adding a little cooking water to loosen. Stir through the whole peas and Parmesan, spoon into serving bowls, top with dollops of the pea purée, the ricotta, crumble over the bacon and serve with extra mint leaves and Parmesan.

 Melting Pea and Pesto Fusilli with Bacon and Ricotta Cook the fusilli as above. Add the peas to the pan 2–3 minutes before the end of the cooking time and cook until tender. Meanwhile, cook the bacon as above. Drain the pasta and peas, return to the pan and stir through 5 table-spoons shop-bought green pesto. Cut 125 g (4 oz) mozzarella into chunks and stir in the pasta until starting to melt. Serve, scattered with the bacon and ricotta as above.

Pea, Bacon and Ricotta Pasta Bakes Cook 325 g (11 oz) angel hair pasta according to the pack instructions. Add the peas to the pan 2–3 minutes before the end of the cooking time and cook until just tender. Drain, then cool under cold running water and drain again. Mix together 250 g (8 oz) ricotta, 5 beaten eggs, 3 crumbled grilled bacon rashers, the grated rind of 1 lemon and a handful of chopped basil leaves in a large bowl, then stir in the pasta and peas. Grease 12 holes of a muffin tin, then divide the mixture between the holes. Top with 25 g (1 oz) grated Cheddar cheese and place in a preheated oven, 200°C (400°F), Gas Mark 6, for 15 minutes or until golden and cooked through.

Tomato Soup with Pasta Shapes

Serves 4

2 tablespoons olive oil
1 onion, finely chopped
1 carrot, peeled and finely
  chopped
1 celery stick, finely chopped
2 teaspoons tomato purée
400 g (13 oz) can chopped
  tomatoes
1 teaspoon sugar
250 ml (8 fl oz) hot vegetable
  stock
handful of basil leaves, chopped
100 g (3½ oz) alphabet pasta
salt

· Heat the oil in a large saucepan, add the vegetables and cook for 5 minutes until softened. Add the tomato purée, tomatoes, sugar and stock and bring to the boil. Reduce the heat, then simmer for 12 minutes.

· Stir in the basil, then remove the pan from the heat. Using a stick blender, whizz together to form a smooth soup.

· Meanwhile, cook the pasta in a large saucepan of salted boiling water for 2 minutes less than directed on the pack instructions. Drain, then stir into the soup and return to the heat.

· Simmer for another couple of minutes or until the pasta is cooked through. Ladle into serving bowls.

Quick Rocket and Tomato Pasta Shapes Heat a little olive oil in a large saucepan, add 1 chopped garlic clove and gently cook until softened. Add 100 g (3½ oz) alphabet or stelline pasta, then stir in 150 ml (¼ pint) hot vegetable stock and 2 chopped tomatoes. Bring to the boil, then cover with a lid and simmer for 5 minutes or until the pasta is cooked through and the liquid has been absorbed. Toss through a handful of rocket leaves, then serve immediately.

Fresh Tomato Soup with Pasta Shapes Place 1 kg (2 lb) tomatoes in a heatproof bowl and pour over boiling water to cover. Leave for 1–2 minutes, then drain, cut a cross at the stem end of each tomato and peel off the skins. Halve the tomatoes, remove the seeds and roughly chop. Make the tomato soup as above, replacing the canned tomatoes with the fresh tomatoes and adding a little more stock to the soup if needed.

PAS-FAMI-BEO

Ham and Courgette Lasagne

Serves 4

500 ml (17 fl oz) shop-bought
   tomato pasta sauce
6 slices of ham, cut into
   bite-sized pieces
handful of basil leaves, chopped
1 courgette, grated
8 fresh lasagne sheets
150 ml (¼ pint) crème fraîche
6 tablespoons water
25 g (1 oz) Parmesan cheese,
   grated
salt and pepper

- Place the tomato pasta sauce in a saucepan and heat through, then stir in the ham, basil and courgette and season.

- Meanwhile, prepare the lasagne sheets, if necessary, according to the pack instructions. Mix together the crème fraîche and measurement water in a bowl until smooth.

- Spread a third of the tomato sauce over the bottom of a medium-sized ovenproof dish. Drizzle a quarter of the crème fraîche over the sauce, then top with a third of the lasagne sheets, cutting to fit the dish, if necessary. Repeat with the remaining ingredients, finishing with the remaining crème fraîche, and scatter with the Parmesan.

- Place in a preheated oven, 200°C (400°F), Gas Mark 6, for 15 minutes or until bubbling and cooked through.

1 **Parma Ham and Courgette Open Lasagne** Cook 8 fresh lasagne sheets in a large saucepan of salted boiling water for 3–5 minutes or until soft, then drain well and cut into squares. Meanwhile, heat the courgette and basil in the tomato pasta sauce as above, adding 4 slices of chopped Parma ham. Pile up the lasagne squares on a plate, layering with the tomato sauce. Serve topped with a dollop of crème fraîche.

2 **Bacon and Courgette Linguine** Cook 400 g (13 oz) linguine according to the pack instructions until al dente. Meanwhile, cut 2 courgettes into thick slices. Cook under a preheated medium grill with 6 bacon rashers for 5–10 minutes, turning once, until golden and cooked through. Place 50 ml (2 fl oz) double cream and the grated rind of 1 lemon in a small saucepan and cook until reduced a little. Drain the pasta and return to the pan. Slice the bacon rashers, then stir through the pasta with the cream, grilled courgettes and bacon and a handful of rocket leaves. Serve immediately.

20 Chicken Fettuccine Alfredo

Serves 4

2 boneless, skinless chicken
  breasts
400 g (13 oz) fettuccine
25 g (1 oz) butter
125 ml (4 fl oz) single cream
50 g (2 oz) Parmesan cheese,
  grated
salt and pepper
finely sliced chives, to garnish

- Place the chicken breasts in a small pan, pour over enough water to cover and simmer for 12–15 minutes or until just cooked through.

- Meanwhile, cook the pasta in a large saucepan of salted boiling water according to the pack instructions until al dente.

- Melt the butter in a separate saucepan, then stir in the cream and simmer for 1–2 minutes and season well. Using a fork, break the chicken into bite-sized pieces.

- Drain the pasta, reserving a little of the cooking water, and return to the pan. Toss through the chicken, creamy sauce and Parmesan, adding a little cooking water to loosen if needed. Season well.

- Spoon into serving bowls and serve sprinkled with the chives.

10 Quick Chicken Spaghetti Alfredo

Cook 400 g (13 oz) quick-cook spaghetti and the cream sauce as above. Drain the pasta, reserving a little of the cooking water, and return to the pan. Toss through 2 shop-bought roasted chicken breasts, skin discarded and torn into shreds, the sauce and Parmesan as above. Serve immediately.

30 Chicken Fettuccine in a White Wine

Sauce Melt 25 g (1 oz) butter, then add 1 sliced red onion and cook over a low heat for 15 minutes until very soft and lightly browned. Pour over 75 ml (3 fl oz) dry white wine and cook for a further 5–10 minutes until reduced down. Pour over 125 ml (4 fl oz) double cream and simmer for 1–2 minutes. Meanwhile, cook the chicken and fettuccine as above. Drain the pasta and stir through the chicken, cut into bite-sized pieces, and wine sauce. Serve immediately.

Pasta Rolls with Red Pepper and Ricotta

Serves 4

8 dried lasagne sheets
500 g (1 lb) ricotta cheese
75 g (3 oz) Parmesan cheese, grated
2 roasted red peppers from a jar, drained and cut into strips
350 ml (12 fl oz) shop-bought tomato pasta sauce
oil, for greasing
150 g (5 oz) cherry tomatoes, halved
salt

- Cook the lasagne sheets in a large saucepan of salted boiling water for 6 minutes, then drain. Cool under cold running water and drain again.

- Spread ricotta over a lasagne sheet and sprinkle with a little of the Parmesan. Arrange a couple of strips of red pepper on top, then roll up tightly to form a tube. Cut into small cylinders, about 2 cm (¾ inch) long. Repeat with the remaining lasagne sheets.

- Pour the tomato pasta sauce over a large, lightly greased ovenproof dish. Arrange the pasta rolls on top. Tuck the tomatoes into any gaps, then scatter over the remaining Parmesan.

- Place in a preheated oven, 200°C (400°F), Gas Mark 6, for 15 minutes or until the pasta is soft and the sauce is bubbling.

1 **Easy Red Pepper and Ricotta Pasta Salad** Cook 500 g (1 lb) fresh conchiglie according to the pack instructions until al dente. Meanwhile, place 2 drained roasted red peppers from a jar, 2 deseeded tomatoes, 1 crushed garlic clove, a handful of basil leaves and 3 tablespoons extra virgin olive oil in a food processor or blender and whizz together. Drain the pasta, then tip into a serving dish and stir through the red pepper sauce. Serve with 125 g (4 oz) ricotta cheese dolloped over.

2 **Pasta Rolls with Courgettes and Ricotta** Make the recipe as above, replacing the red peppers with 2 courgettes, cut into thin strips. Rub the courgette strips with 2 tablespoons olive oil, then cook under a preheated medium grill for 2–3 minutes on each side until lightly charred and soft. Arrange on the lasagne sheets with the cheese and then cook as above.

Farfalle with Chicken Sweetcorn Bites and Red Pepper Sauce

Serves 4

300 g (10 oz) minced chicken

2 spring onions, finely chopped

1 egg yolk

25 g (1 oz) fresh white breadcrumbs

50 g (2 oz) frozen sweetcorn, thawed

4 tablespoons olive oil, plus extra for greasing

400 g (13 oz) farfalle

3 ready-roasted red peppers

handful of basil leaves, chopped, plus extra to garnish (optional)

salt and pepper

- Mix together the chicken, spring onions, egg yolk, breadcrumbs and sweetcorn in a bowl, then season well. Lightly wet your hands, then shape the mixture into small balls, each about the size of a walnut.

- Place the chicken balls on a greased baking sheet and drizzle over 1 tablespoon of the oil. Place in a preheated oven, 200°C (400°F), Gas Mark 6, for 12–15 minutes, turning once, until cooked through.

- Meanwhile, cook the pasta in a saucepan of salted boiling water according to the pack instructions until al dente.

- Place the red peppers, 2 tablespoons of the oil and the basil in a food processor or blender and whizz together to form a chunky sauce. Drain the pasta, reserving a little of the cooking water, and return to the pan. Stir through the remaining oil and the red pepper sauce, adding a little cooking water to loosen if needed. Spoon into bowls, add the chicken bites, scatter over some basil and serve.

---

10 **Chicken, Sweetcorn and Red Pepper Pasta Salad** Cook 300 g (10 oz) orzo according to the pack instructions, adding 100 g (3½ oz) canned sweetcorn 1 minute before the end of the cooking time. Drain, cool under cold running water and drain again. Tip into a serving dish and mix with 1 shop-bought roasted chicken breast, skin discarded and flesh torn into shreds, 5 tablespoons mayonnaise, 1 cored, deseeded and chopped red pepper and a handful of chopped basil leaves.

30 **Chicken and Sweetcorn Farfalle with Red Pepper Sauce** Heat 4 tablespoons olive oil in a frying pan, add 2 sliced garlic cloves and cook for 30 seconds. Stir in 4 cored, deseeded and chopped red peppers, reduce the heat to low and cook for 15 minutes or until softened. Pour over 200 ml (7 fl oz) passata and cook for a further 10 minutes until thickened. Meanwhile, fry 2 seasoned boneless, skinless chicken breasts in a little olive oil for 7 minutes on each side or until golden and cooked through, then remove from the pan. Add 50 g (2 oz) frozen sweetcorn, thawed, and cook for 1–2 minutes until lightly browned. Cut the chicken into slices. While the peppers and chicken are cooking, cook and drain the farfalle as above. Stir through the chicken slices and red pepper sauce, then serve topped with the sweetcorn and sprinkled with chopped basil leaves.

30 Seafood Spaghetti in a Creamy Sauce

Serves 4

15 g (½ oz) butter
1 shallot, finely chopped
100 ml (3½ fl oz) dry vermouth
200 ml (7 fl oz) hot fish stock
300 g (10 oz) salmon fillet
75 g (3 oz) small cooked
    unpeeled prawns
12 scallops, corals removed
150 ml (¼ pint) double cream
handful of chives, chopped, plus
    extra to garnish
400 g (13 oz) spaghetti
salt and pepper

- Melt the butter in a saucepan, add the shallot and cook for 3 minutes until softened. Pour over the vermouth and bubble for 5 minutes until reduced by half. Add the stock, then place the salmon in the pan, making sure it is covered with liquid, and gently poach for 5–10 minutes or until the fish is cooked through and flakes easily. Remove from the pan, discard the skin and flake into bite-sized pieces.

- Add the prawns to the pan, then add the scallops and cook for a further 2 minutes or until just cooked through. Set aside with the salmon.

- Add the cream to the pan and bubble until reduced down to a sauce, then season. Carefully stir in the reserved seafood, heat through and add the chives.

- Meanwhile, cook the pasta in a large saucepan of salted boiling water according to the pack instructions until al dente. Drain, then toss through the seafood sauce and season. Serve sprinkled with extra chopped chives.

---

1 Simple Seafood Spaghetti

Cook the spaghetti as above. Add 200 g (7 oz) large raw peeled prawns 3 minutes and 100 g (3½ oz) frozen peas to the pan 2–3 minutes before the end of the cooking time and cook until the prawns turn pink and are cooked through and the peas are tender. Drain well and return to the pan, then stir through 100 g (3½ oz) crème fraîche and a handful of chopped dill. Serve at once.

2 Seafood Spaghetti with Parma Ham

Cook the spaghetti as above. Meanwhile, melt a little butter in a large frying pan, add 4 sliced spring onions and cook for a couple of minutes until softened. Add 8 large scallops, corals removed, and a handful of large raw peeled prawns, season and cook over a medium-high heat for 2 minutes on each side or until the prawns have turned pink and the scallops are golden. Remove from the pan. Stir in a splash of dry white wine and bubble until reduced, then add 100 ml (3½ fl oz) double cream and mix in the seafood to warm through. Heat 1 teaspoon olive oil in a separate frying pan, add 2 slices of Parma ham and cook for 1–2 minutes or until browned. Drain the pasta and stir into the seafood sauce, then crumble over the Parma ham. Serve immediately.

Chicken Parmigiana with Tomato Fusilli Lunghi

Serves 4

100 g (3½ oz) fresh white breadcrumbs

25 g (1 oz) Parmesan cheese, grated

4 tablespoons olive oil, plus extra for greasing

4 small boneless, skinless chicken breasts

75 g (3 oz) mozzarella cheese, cut into 4 slices

300 g (10 oz) fusilli lunghi

250 ml (8 fl oz) shop-bought tomato pasta sauce

salt and pepper

green salad, to serve

· Mix together the breadcrumbs and Parmesan on a large plate and season. Rub about 2 teaspoons of the oil over each chicken breast, press down with your palm to flatten a little, then dip in the breadcrumb mixture until coated all over. Place on a lightly greased grill pan.

· Drizzle with a little more oil, then cook under a preheated hot grill for 10 minutes, turning once, until golden and cooked through. Top each chicken breast with a slice of mozzarella and cook for a further 2 minutes or until the cheese has melted.

· Meanwhile, cook the pasta in a large saucepan of salted boiling water according to the pack instructions until al dente. Heat the tomato pasta sauce in a small saucepan. Drain the pasta and toss through the sauce. Cut each chicken breast in half. Spoon into serving bowls and top with the grilled chicken. Serve with the green salad.

Easy Chicken, Mozzarella and Tomato Spaghetti Heat 1 tablespoon olive oil in a wok or large frying pan, add 300 g (10 oz) stir-fry chicken strips and stir-fry for 7 minutes or until just cooked through. Pour over 250 ml (8 fl oz) shop-bought tomato pasta sauce and simmer for 1–2 minutes. Meanwhile, cook 400 g (13 oz) spaghetti according to the pack instructions until al dente. Drain and return to the pan. Cut 75 g (3 oz) mozzarella cheese into small chunks and stir through the pasta with the chicken sauce. Serve immediately.

Chicken, Mozzarella and Tomato Pasta Bake Cook 400 g (13 oz) fusilli according to the pack instructions until al dente. Drain and return to the pan. Toss through 250 ml (8 fl oz) shop-bought tomato pasta sauce and 2 shop-bought roasted chicken breasts, skin discarded and flesh cut into bite-sized pieces. Tip into an ovenproof dish. Mix together 150 g (5 oz) crème fraîche with enough milk to make a sauce, then drizzle over the top of the pasta. Scatter with 125 g (4 oz) grated mozzarella and place in a preheated oven, 200°C (400°F), Gas Mark 6, for 15 minutes or until golden and bubbling.

Creamy Mustard and Sausage Pasta

Serves 4

2 tablespoons olive oil
6 pork sausages
1 onion, thickly sliced
2 teaspoons wholegrain mustard
150 ml (¼ pint) hot vegetable or
  chicken stock
75 g (3 oz) crème fraîche
juice and grated rind of ½ lemon
400 g (13 oz) chifferi pasta
salt
chopped flat-leaf parsley,
  to garnish

- Brush a little oil over each sausage, then cook under a preheated medium grill for 15 minutes or until golden and cooked through. Cool slightly, then cut into bite-sized pieces.

- Meanwhile, heat the remaining oil in a pan, add the onion and cook for 10 minutes until softened. Stir in the mustard and stock and simmer for 5 minutes, then stir in the crème fraîche and lemon juice and most of the rind.

- While the sausages and sauce are cooking, cook the pasta in a large saucepan of salted boiling water according to the pack instructions until al dente. Drain, reserving a little of the cooking water, and return to the pan. Stir through the sausages and sauce, adding a little cooking water to loosen if needed.

- Spoon into serving bowls and serve sprinkled with the parsley and the remaining lemon rind.

Quick Mustard and Pancetta Pasta

Cook and drain the chifferi pasta as above. Meanwhile, heat a little olive oil in a frying pan, add 150 g (5 oz) pancetta cubes and 2 sliced garlic cloves and cook for 5 minutes. Stir in 2 teaspoons wholegrain mustard and 75 g (3 oz) crème fraîche. Stir through the drained pasta and serve as above.

Slow-Cooked Onion and Mustardy Sausage Pasta

Heat a little olive oil in a frying pan, add 1 sliced red onion and cook over a low heat for 20–25 minutes until soft and golden. Meanwhile, grill the sausages as above and cut into bite-sized pieces. Stir into the onion with 1 chopped garlic clove, a splash of dry white wine, 1 chopped sage leaf and 2 teaspoons wholegrain mustard. Simmer for 5 minutes, then stir in 2 tablespoons crème fraîche. Meanwhile, cook and drain the chifferi pasta as above. Stir through the sauce and serve immediately.

Simple One-Pan Tomato Pasta

Serves 4

4 tablespoons olive oil
350 g (11 ½ oz) garganelli pasta
thyme sprig, leaves stripped and
  chopped
4 tablespoons tomato purée
2 teaspoons red wine vinegar
2.5 litres (4 pints) hot chicken
  stock
pinch of caster sugar
125 g (4 oz) cherry tomatoes,
  halved
salt and pepper
chopped basil leaves, to garnish
Parmesan cheese shavings,
  to serve

- Heat the oil in a large, deep flameproof casserole, add the pasta and toss around the pan for a couple of minutes until golden. Add the thyme, tomato purée and vinegar and stir in to coat the pasta.

- Add a ladleful of stock and the sugar to the pan. Keeping the sauce at a gentle simmer, add the stock, one ladleful at a time, stirring occasionally.

- After 10 minutes cooking, add the tomatoes. Cook for a further 5–10 minutes until the liquid has been absorbed or the pasta is tender. Season well and serve scattered with the basil and Parmesan shavings.

1 **Penne with Sun-Dried Tomato and Basil Pesto** Cook 400 g (13 oz) penne according to the pack instructions until al dente. Meanwhile, place 50 g (2 oz) drained sun-dried tomatoes in oil, 2 crushed garlic cloves, 25 g (1 oz) toasted pine nuts, 1 teaspoon balsamic vinegar, 3 tablespoons extra virgin olive oil and a handful of basil leaves in a food processor or blender and whizz together to form a pesto. Drain the pasta, reserving a little of the cooking water, and return to the pan. Stir through the pesto, adding a little cooking water to loosen if needed. Serve immediately.

3 **Slow-Cooked Tomato Pasta** Halve and deseed 250 g (8 oz) plum tomatoes. Place in a large frying pan with 125 ml (4 fl oz) olive oil and 3 garlic cloves and cook over a very low heat for 20–25 minutes until soft and just about to fall apart. Season well. Meanwhile, cook and drain the garganelli as above. Stir through the tomatoes with a handful of chopped basil leaves and a handful of grated Parmesan cheese. Serve immediately.

Easy Sausage Spaghetti Bolognese

Serves 4

1 tablespoon olive oil
6 garlic sausages
1 onion, finely chopped
150 g (5 oz) button mushrooms,
  quartered
1 teaspoon tomato purée
400 g (13 oz) can chopped
  tomatoes
handful of basil leaves, finely
  chopped
125 ml (4 fl oz) water
400 g (13 oz) spaghetti
salt and pepper
grated Parmesan cheese,
  to serve

- Heat a large frying pan until hot, then add the oil.
  Remove the sausages from their casings and crumble the
  sausagemeat into the pan. Cook for a couple of minutes,
  breaking up the meat with the back of a spoon. When it
  begins to colour, add the onion and cook for a further
  5 minutes. Stir in the mushrooms and cook until they begin
  to soften.

- Stir in the tomato purée, tomatoes, basil and measurement
  water. Bring to the boil, then reduce the heat and simmer
  for 10 minutes or until cooked through. Season well.

- Meanwhile, cook the pasta in a large saucepan of salted
  boiling water according to the pack instructions until al
  dente, then drain. Spoon into serving bowls and top with
  the sausage sauce. Serve scattered with the Parmesan.

10 **Simple Bacon Spaghetti**
Bolognese Cook and drain the
spaghetti as above. Meanwhile,
heat a little olive oil in a frying
pan, add 3 finely sliced bacon
rashers and cook for 1–2
minutes. Pour over 350 ml
(12 fl oz) shop-bought Bolognese
pasta sauce, then stir in a 250 g
(8 oz) pouch ready-cooked Puy
lentils. Simmer for 5 minutes,
then toss through the drained
pasta. Serve immediately.

30 **Sausage Meatball Spaghetti**
Bolognese Remove the
sausages from their casings
as above and place in a bowl.
Lightly wet your hands, then
shape the sausagemeat into
small balls. Cook in the oil as
above, adding the onion, but
omitting the mushrooms. Stir in
75 ml (3 fl oz) dry white wine and
simmer until nearly cooked away,
then add the tomato purée,
tomatoes and measurement
water and continue as above.

Frying Pan Macaroni Cheese

Serves 4

325 g (11 oz) macaroni
50 g (2 oz) butter
50 g (2 oz) plain flour
600 ml (1 pint) milk
100 g (3½ oz) Cheddar cheese, grated
25 g (1 oz) dried white breadcrumbs
25 g (1 oz) Parmesan cheese, grated
salt and pepper

· Cook the pasta in a large saucepan of salted boiling water according to the pack instructions until al dente.

· Meanwhile, melt the butter in a large, ovenproof frying pan and stir in the flour to make a smooth paste. Cook until golden, then gradually whisk in the milk. Bring to the boil over a medium heat, then simmer for about 3 minutes until slightly thickened. Remove from the heat, stir in the cheese and season.

· Drain the pasta, then tip into the frying pan. Stir into the cheese sauce until well combined. Scatter over the breadcrumbs and Parmesan.

· Place in a preheated oven, 190°C (375°F), Gas Mark 5, for 15 minutes or until golden brown and bubbling.

1 **Pasta in a Cheesy Sauce** Cook 400 g (13 oz) chifferi pasta according to the pack instructions until al dente. Meanwhile, place 1 garlic clove and 100 ml (3½ fl oz) double cream in a saucepan and cook for 5 minutes. Remove and discard the garlic and stir in 50 g (2 oz) grated Parmesan cheese. Drain the pasta and return to the pan. Stir through the sauce and serve immediately.

2 **Creamy Macaroni Cheese** Melt a little butter in a saucepan, add 1 finely chopped shallot and cook until softened. Pour over 75 ml (3 fl oz) dry white wine and cook for 5–10 minutes until reduced down. Stir through 150 g (5 oz) crème fraîche and enough milk to make a smooth sauce. Meanwhile, cook and drain the macaroni as above. Tip into a heatproof dish and stir through the sauce. Scatter over 50 g (2 oz) grated Gruyère cheese and cook under a preheated medium grill for 7 minutes or until golden and bubbling.

Tagliarelle with Pesto and Charred Tomatoes

Serves 4

250 g (8 oz) cherry tomatoes
1 tablespoon olive oil
400 g (13 oz) tagliarelle
5 tablespoons shop-bought fresh
   green pesto
3 tablespoons mascarpone
   cheese
2 tablespoons toasted pine nuts
salt and pepper

- Place the cherry tomatoes on a baking sheet, then mix together with the oil and season. Cook under a preheated medium grill for 5 minutes or until beginning to brown.

- Meanwhile, cook the pasta in a large saucepan of salted boiling water according to the pack instructions until al dente. Drain, reserving a little of the cooking water, and return to the pan. Stir through the pesto and mascarpone, adding a little cooking water to loosen if needed.

- Gently stir in the tomatoes and season. Spoon into serving bowls and serve with the pine nuts scattered over.

---

2 **Tomato Tagliarelle with Pesto-stuffed Chicken** Mix together 4 tablespoons shop-bought fresh green pesto and 2 tablespoons mascarpone cheese in a bowl, then spoon under the skin of 4 boneless chicken breasts. Place in a roasting tin and drizzle with olive oil. Place in a preheated oven, 220°C (425°F), Gas Mark 7, and cook for 15 minutes. Add a handful of cherry tomatoes, return to the oven and cook for a further 5 minutes or until the chicken is cooked through and the tomatoes have softened. Meanwhile, cook and drain 300 g (10 oz) tagliarelle as above, then stir through the tomatoes and 3 tablespoons mascarpone. Serve with the chicken.

---

3 **Mexican-Style Tagliarelle with Spicy Tomato Pesto** Heat a little olive oil in a frying pan, add 1 sliced onion and cook over a low heat for 10 minutes until softened. Drain a 400 g (13 oz) can cannellini beans and add to the onion. Pour over 100 ml (3½ fl oz) hot chicken stock and simmer for 15 minutes until all the liquid has been absorbed. Meanwhile, place 25 g (1 oz) pumpkin seeds, 1 jalapeno chilli, 2 drained sun-dried tomatoes in oil, a handful of coriander leaves and a squeeze of lime juice in a small food processor or blender and whizz together to form a pesto. Cook and drain the tagliarelle as above. Stir through the beans and 3 tablespoons soured cream. Serve topped with the pesto.

Broccoli and Ham Pasta Bake

Serves 4

400 g (13 oz) spirali
125 g (4 oz) tenderstem broccoli
450 ml (¾ pint) hot chicken or
  vegetable stock
1 teaspoon mustard
200 g (7 oz) crème fraîche
150 g (5 oz) ham, cut into
  bite-sized pieces
125 g (4 oz) Cheddar cheese,
  grated
salt and pepper

- Cook the pasta in a large saucepan of salted boiling water according to the pack instructions until al dente. Add the broccoli 5 minutes before the end of the cooking time and cook until just tender. Drain and return to the pan.

- Meanwhile, stir together the stock, mustard and crème fraîche in a jug, then mix together with the pasta, broccoli, ham and half the Cheddar and season. Spoon into an ovenproof dish and scatter over the remaining cheese.

- Place in a preheated oven, 200°C (400°F), Gas Mark 6, for 15 minutes or until golden, bubbling and cooked through.

Quick Broccoli and Ham Cavatappi

Cook 500 g (1 lb) fresh cavatappi according to the pack instructions until al dente, adding the broccoli as above. Meanwhile, heat a little olive oil in a frying pan, add 1 garlic clove and cook for 30 seconds. Pour over 150 ml (¼ pint) passata and simmer for 5 minutes. Drain the pasta and broccoli and return to the pan. Stir through the tomato sauce and the ham as above and serve scattered with grated Parmesan cheese.

Ham, Broccoli and Spirali Gratin

Cook the spirali and broccoli as above, adding 250 g (8 oz) baby spinach leaves to the pan just before draining. Drain the pasta and vegetables and return to the pan. Mix together with 200 ml (7 fl oz) hot chicken or vegetable stock and the crème fraîche and ham as above. Tip into a heatproof dish and scatter over 125 g (4 oz) sliced mozzarella. Cook under a preheated medium grill for 5–10 minutes or until golden and bubbling.

Salmon and Leek Conchiglie

Serves 4

2 x 150 g (5 oz) salmon fillets
2 tablespoons butter
2 leeks, trimmed, cleaned and
    finely sliced
juice and grated rind of 1 lemon
400 g (13 oz) conchiglie
50 ml (2 fl oz) soured cream
salt and pepper

- Place the salmon fillets in a frying pan and pour over enough water to cover. Bring to the boil, then reduce the heat and simmer for 10 minutes or until the fish is cooked through and flakes easily. Remove the skin and any bones and use a fork to break into large chunks.

- Meanwhile, heat the butter in a small saucepan, add the leeks and cook over a gentle heat for 10 minutes or until softened and cooked through. Stir in the lemon juice and most of the rind.

- Cook the pasta in a large saucepan of salted boiling water according to the pack instructions until al dente. Drain, reserving a little of the cooking water, and return to the pan. Stir through the salmon and leeks and season, then stir in the soured cream, adding a little cooking water if needed to make a sauce. Serve immediately with plenty of black pepper and the remaining lemon rind scattered over.

Simple Salmon and Leek Conchiglie

Cook 500 g (1 lb) fresh conchiglie according to the pack instructions until al dente. Add the leeks, prepared as above, to the pan 3 minutes before the end of the cooking time and cook until softened. Drain and return to the pan. Stir in 150 g (5 oz) sliced smoked salmon with the soured cream and lemon juice as above. Serve immediately.

Salmon, Smoked Haddock and Leek

Pasta Bake Poach 1 smoked haddock fillet and 1 salmon fillet in 200 ml (7 fl oz) milk for 10 minutes or until the fish is cooked through and flakes easily. Remove any skin and bones and flake into small pieces. Meanwhile, cook the leeks and pasta as above, adding 200 g (7 oz) baby spinach leaves to the pasta just before draining. Stir in the fish and poaching liquid, leeks and 50 g (2 oz) crème fraîche, then spoon into an ovenproof dish. Sprinkle over 25 g (1 oz) fresh white breadcrumbs and dab over a little butter, then place in a preheated oven, 200°C (400°F), Gas Mark 6, for 15 minutes or until golden and cooked through.

Tuna and Sweetcorn Pasta Bake

Serves 4

40 g (1½ oz) butter
40 g (1½ oz) plain flour
575 ml (18 fl oz) milk
400 g (13 oz) fusilli
2 x 185 g (6½ oz) cans tuna in
  spring water, drained
200 g (7 oz) can sweetcorn,
  drained
75 g (3 oz) Cheddar cheese,
  grated
25 g (1 oz) dried white
  breadcrumbs
salt and pepper

· Melt the butter in a medium-sized saucepan and stir
  in the flour to make a smooth paste. Cook until golden,
  then gradually whisk in the milk. Bring to the boil, stirring
  constantly, then reduce the heat and simmer for 10 minutes
  until thickened, stirring occasionally. Season well.

· Meanwhile, cook the pasta in a large saucepan of salted
  boiling water according to the pack instructions until al dente.
  Drain and return to the pan. Mix in the white sauce, tuna,
  sweetcorn and the Cheddar, reserving a little for the topping.

· Spoon into a medium ovenproof dish and sprinkle with the
  breadcrumbs and reserved cheese. Place in a preheated
  oven, 200°C (400°F), Gas Mark 6, for 15 minutes or until
  lightly browned and bubbling.

Tuna and Sweetcorn Pasta Salad Cook 300 g (10 oz) fusilli as above. Drain, then cool under cold running water and drain again. Tip into a serving dish and stir through 6 tablespoons mayonnaise, a drained 185 g (6½ oz) can tuna in spring water and 125 g (4 oz) drained canned sweetcorn.

Creamy Sweetcorn and Bacon Fusilli Heat a little olive oil in a frying pan, add 1 finely chopped onion and cook until beginning to soften. Cut 4 bacon rashers into small pieces, add to the pan and cook for 5–7 minutes or until the bacon is golden and cooked through. Pour over 100 ml (3½ fl oz) hot vegetable stock and cook for a further 5 minutes until beginning to reduce. Add a drained 200 g (7 oz) can sweetcorn and 50 ml (2 fl oz) double cream and cook for 5 minutes or until the sweetcorn is cooked through. Meanwhile, cook and drain the fusilli as above. Stir through the sauce with 25 g (1 oz) grated Cheddar cheese. Serve immediately.

Linguine Fiorentina with Ham

Serves 4

1 tablespoon olive oil
1 onion, finely chopped
2 garlic cloves, finely chopped
200 g (7 oz) spinach leaves,
  chopped
75 g (3 oz) low-fat crème fraîche
handful of grated Parmesan
  cheese, plus extra to serve
400 g (13 oz) linguine
100 g (3½ oz) smoked ham, sliced
salt and pepper

· Heat the oil in a frying pan, add the onion and garlic and cook for 5 minutes until softened.

· Place the spinach in a colander over the sink and pour over enough boiling water until just wilted. Squeeze out any excess water. Place in a food processor or blender with the onion and garlic, crème fraîche and Parmesan and whizz together to form a thick paste. Set aside.

· Cook the pasta in a large saucepan of salted boiling water according to the pack instructions until al dente. Drain, reserving a little of the cooking water, and return to the pan. Stir through the spinach mixture, adding a little cooking water to loosen.

· Stir through the ham and season. Spoon into serving bowls and serve scattered with extra Parmesan.

Mushroom, Spinach and Ham Linguine

Heat a little olive oil in a frying pan, add 1 sliced garlic clove and 150 g (5 oz) mixed wild mushrooms, trimmed and halved if large, and cook for 3 minutes until soft. Cook the linguine as above, adding 200 g (7 oz) baby spinach leaves just before draining. Drain and return to the pan. Stir through the mushrooms, 100 g (3½ oz) sliced ham and 3 tablespoons crème fraîche. Serve as above.

Linguine Fiorentina Ham and Egg Bakes

Cook the recipe as above, then divide the mixture between 4 large individual soufflé dishes. Crack an egg over each one and top with a little butter. Place in a preheated oven, 180°C (350°F), Gas Mark 4, for 10 minutes or until the eggs are just cooked through. Serve immediately.

 # Spinach and Ricotta Cannelloni

Serves 4

250 g (8 oz) spinach leaves
handful of basil leaves
500 g (1 lb) ricotta cheese
50 g (2 oz) Parmesan cheese, grated
pinch of grated nutmeg
500 ml (17 fl oz) shop-bought tomato pasta sauce
8 fresh lasagne sheets
125 g (4 oz) mozzarella cheese, thinly sliced
salt and pepper
green salad, to serve (optional)

- Place the spinach in a colander over the sink and pour over enough boiling water until just wilted. Squeeze out any excess water. Roughly chop the spinach and basil, place in a bowl and mix together with the ricotta, half the Parmesan and the nutmeg. Season to taste.

- Heat the tomato pasta sauce in a small saucepan until simmering.

- Prepare the lasagne sheets, if necessary, according to the pack instructions. Spread about a third of the tomato sauce over the bottom of a medium-sized ovenproof dish. Spoon 2–3 tablespoons of the spinach mixture along the length of each sheet. Roll up and place in the dish. Pour over the remaining tomato sauce and arrange the mozzarella on top.

- Scatter over the remaining Parmesan and place in a preheated oven, 200°C (400°F), Gas Mark 6, for 15–20 minutes until the cheese is golden. Serve with green salad, if liked.

---

1 Spinach Spaghetti with Ricotta

Cook 400 g (13 oz) spaghetti according to the pack instructions until al dente. Drain and return to the pan. Toss through 200 g (7 oz) chopped spinach, 4 tablespoons shop-bought fresh green pesto and a handful of halved baby plum tomatoes. Top with dollops of ricotta cheese and serve with grated Parmesan cheese, if liked.

2 Quick Spinach and Ricotta Lasagne

Cook 8 fresh lasagne sheets in a large saucepan of salted boiling water for 3–5 minutes or until soft, then drain well. Prepare 100 g (3½ oz) spinach leaves as above, drain well, then finely chop and mix together with half the tomato pasta sauce and 3 tablespoons shop-bought fresh green pesto. Spoon a layer of the spinach mixture into a heatproof dish and cover with a layer of lasagne sheets. Spoon 250 g (8 oz) ricotta on top, then cover with another layer of pasta. Pour over the remaining tomato sauce, grate over 25 g (1 oz) Parmesan cheese and cook under a preheated medium grill for 10 minutes or until golden and cooked through.

Hearty Sausage and Spinach Pasta Bake

Serves 4

6 large pork sausages
1 tablespoon olive oil
500 ml (17 fl oz) shop-bought tomato pasta sauce
300 g (10 oz) penne
200 g (7 oz) baby spinach leaves
250 g (8 oz) ricotta cheese
200 g (7 oz) mascarpone cheese
5 tablespoons milk
125 g (4 oz) mozzarella cheese, torn
salt and pepper

· Squeeze the sausages out of their casings into a bowl. Lightly wet your hands, then shape the sausagemeat into tiny meatballs. Heat the oil in a frying pan, add the sausage balls and cook for about 5 minutes, stirring frequently, until golden all over. Pour over the tomato pasta sauce and simmer for 5 minutes.

· Meanwhile, cook the pasta in a large saucepan of salted boiling water according to the pack instructions until al dente. Remove from the heat, add the spinach leaves and then drain, reserving a little of the cooking water, and return to the pan.

· Mix together the ricotta, mascarpone and milk in a bowl, then stir through the pasta and season well.

· Spoon the tomato and sausage sauce into a medium-sized ovenproof dish. Arrange the pasta on top and cover with the mozzarella. Place in a preheated oven, 190 °C (375 °F), Gas Mark 5, for 15 minutes or until golden, bubbling and cooked through.

---

1 **Bacon and Spinach Penne** Cook 4 bacon rashers under a preheated medium grill for 7 minutes or until crisp. Cool for 1 minute, then cut into small pieces. Meanwhile, cook and drain the penne and spinach as above. Toss together with the bacon and 2 chopped tomatoes. Mix 250 g (8 oz) ricotta cheese with 50 g (2 oz) feta cheese in a bowl and spoon over the pasta. Serve immediately.

 2 **Penne with Sausages and Spinach** Heat 2 tablespoons olive oil in a frying pan, add 1 sliced garlic clove and cook for 30 seconds. Pour over a 400 g (13 oz) can chopped tomatoes and a pinch each of dried chilli flakes and dried oregano. Simmer for 15 minutes until thickened. Meanwhile, cook 6 large pork sausages under a preheated medium grill for 15 minutes or until cooked through. Cool

slightly, then cut into bite-sized pieces and heat through in the sauce. Meanwhile, cook and drain the pasta and spinach as above. Toss together with the sausage sauce and then spoon over 125 g (4 oz) ricotta cheese. Serve immediately.

QuickCook
Healthy
Suppers

Recipes listed by cooking time

30

20

Fresh Pasta Broth with Onion Garnish

Serves 4

2 tablespoons olive oil
2 onions, 1 finely chopped and
  1 thinly sliced
2 garlic cloves, finely chopped
2 tablespoons chopped mint
½ teaspoon turmeric
200 g (7 oz) canned chickpeas,
  drained and rinsed
200 g (7 oz) canned kidney
  beans, drained and rinsed
2.5 litres (4 pints) hot
  chicken stock
125 g (4 oz) fine egg noodles,
  broken into small pieces
100 g (3½ oz) frozen peas
100 g (3½ oz) greens, chopped
chopped coriander leaves,
  flat-leaf parsley, to serve

- To make the onion garnish, heat half the oil in a small frying pan, add the thinly sliced onion and cook gently for 10 minutes until softened and lightly golden. Add the garlic and mint and cook for a further minute.

- Meanwhile, heat the oil in a large saucepan, add the chopped onion and cook for a couple of minutes until softened. Stir in the turmeric, then add the chickpeas and kidney beans and stir in the stock. Bring to the boil and cook for a couple of minutes. Add the pasta and cook for a further 5 minutes.

- Add the peas and greens to the soup, season and cook for 2–3 minutes or until the vegetables are tender and the pasta is cooked through.

- Ladle into serving bowls, sprinkle over the onion garnish and chopped herbs, then drizzle with the yogurt. Serve with natural yoghurt and pitta breads.

---

10 **Quick Pasta Broth with Caramelized Onion** Fry 1 teaspoon curry paste in a large saucepan for a couple of seconds, then add 4 tablespoons shop-bought ready-cooked fried onion, pour over the stock as above and bring to the boil. Add 400 g (13 oz) rinsed and drained can chickpeas and the noodles, prepared as above, and simmer until the pasta is cooked. Add the greens and peas 2–3 minutes before the end of cooking time. Serve topped with cooked caramelized onion.

---

30 **Spicy Pasta Pilaff with Crispy Fried Onion** Heat 1 tablespoon olive oil in a large saucepan, add 1 chopped onion and fry gently until softened. Stir in 1 teaspoon ground cumin and a pinch of turmeric. Add 100 g (3½ oz) long grain rice and 100 g (3½ oz) angel hair pasta. Coat in the spices, then pour over 500 ml (17 fl oz) hot chicken stock and add 200 g (7 oz) rinsed and drained canned chickpeas. Bring to the boil, then cover with a lid and simmer for 15–20 minutes or until the rice is just cooked through. Meanwhile, heat a saucepan one-third full of vegetable oil. When hot, fry 1 sliced onion until crisp and browned. Remove with a slotted spoon and serve scattered over the pilaff with chopped mint leaves.

Turkey Meatball and Pasta Soup

Serves 4

500 g (1 lb) minced turkey

50 g (2 oz) fresh white breadcrumbs

25 g (1 oz) Parmesan cheese, grated, plus extra to serve (optional)

2 tablespoons finely chopped flat-leaf parsley, plus extra to garnish

1 egg, lightly beaten

1 garlic clove, crushed

2.5 litres (4 pints) hot chicken stock

2 large carrots, peeled and thinly sliced

175 g (6 oz) farfalline pasta

salt and pepper

- Mix together the turkey, breadcrumbs, Parmesan, parsley, egg and garlic in a large bowl and season to taste. Lightly wet your hands, then shape the mixture into small balls about 2 cm (¾ inch) round.

- Bring the stock to the boil in a large saucepan, then add the carrots and simmer for 5 minutes.

- Drop the turkey meatballs into the stock and cook for 5 minutes. Add the pasta and cook for a further 5–7 minutes or until the meatballs are cooked through. Season to taste.

- Ladle into bowls and serve sprinkled with a little Parmesan and chopped parsley, if liked.

---

1 Simple Turkey Soup Bring 1 litre (1¾ pints) hot chicken stock to the boil, then add 2 peeled and grated carrots and cook for 3 minutes. Stir in the pasta as above and cook for 5–7 minutes or until cooked through, adding 200 g (7 oz) shredded cooked turkey slices 1 minute before the end of the cooking time to heat through. Serve sprinkled with finely chopped dill.

2 Grilled Turkey Steaks with Orzo Dust 4 turkey steaks with a little flour and shake off any excess. Dip into 1 lightly beaten egg. Sprinkle 100 g (3½ oz) dried white breadcrumbs and 25 g (1 oz) grated Parmesan cheese on a plate, then dip in the steaks to coat all over. Brush with a little olive oil and cook under a preheated medium grill for 5–7 minutes on each side or until golden and cooked through. Meanwhile, cut 4 slices of pancetta into matchsticks. Heat a little olive oil in a frying pan and cook for 5 minutes or until golden. Remove from the pan. Tip 1 finely chopped shallot and 1 crushed garlic clove into the frying pan and cook until softened. Cook 150 g (5 oz) thinly sliced carrots for 10 minutes until tender, then add 400 g (13 oz) orzo to the pan and cook according to the pack instructions. Drain and toss together with the pancetta and onion mixture, and serve alongside the turkey steaks.

Rocket, Chilli and Ricotta Spaghetti

Serves 4

400 g (13 oz) spaghetti
1 tablespoon olive oil
1 garlic clove, finely chopped
1 red chilli, deseeded if liked,
   and finely sliced
200 g (7 oz) rocket leaves
150 g (5 oz) ricotta cheese
salt and pepper

- Cook the pasta in a large saucepan of salted boiling water according to the pack instructions until al dente.

- Meanwhile, heat the oil in a small frying pan, add the garlic and chilli and cook for 30 seconds until beginning to brown. Remove from the heat.

- Drain the pasta, reserving a little of the cooking water, and return to the pan. Stir through the chilli oil, adding a little cooking water to loosen if needed. Season well.

- Stir through the rocket, spoon into serving bowls and top with the ricotta. Serve immediately.

Spaghetti with Creamy Ricotta and Salad Leaves Melt 25 g (1 oz) butter in a saucepan and stir in 25 g (1 oz) plain flour to make a smooth paste. Cook until golden, then gradually whisk in 300 ml (½ pint) milk, stirring frequently, and simmer for 5–10 minutes until thickened. Stir in 150 g (5 oz) ricotta cheese and a handful of grated Parmesan cheese. Meanwhile, cook and drain the spaghetti as above. Stir through the ricotta sauce and 200 g (7 oz) mixed baby spinach, rocket and watercress leaves. Serve immediately sprinkled with dried chilli flakes.

Ricotta Pasta Bakes with Spicy Rocket Salad Cook 350 g (11½ oz) angel hair pasta according to the pack instructions. Drain, then cool under cold running water and drain again. Snip into small strips and mix together with 6 beaten eggs and 150 g (5 oz) ricotta cheese in a bowl. Grease 12 holes of a muffin tin, then divide the mixture between the holes. Place in a preheated oven, 200°C (400°F), Gas Mark 6, for 15–20 minutes or until just cooked through. Toss together the rocket and chilli, prepared as above, 1 teaspoon white wine vinegar and 2 tablespoons extra virgin olive oil in a bowl and serve alongside the pasta bakes.

Fettuccine with Goats' Cheese and Tomato Salsa

Serves 4

400 g (13 oz) fettuccine
125 g (4 oz) soft goats' cheese
50 g (2 oz) low-fat cream cheese
salt and pepper

For the tomato salsa

200 g (7 oz) baby plum
   tomatoes, halved
5 sun-dried tomatoes in oil,
   drained and finely chopped
1 tablespoon balsamic vinegar
1 tablespoon extra virgin olive oil
handful of basil leaves, chopped

- To make the tomato salsa, stir together the tomatoes, vinegar, oil and basil in a bowl. Season well and leave to stand for 5 minutes.

- Meanwhile, cook the pasta in a large saucepan of salted boiling water according to the pack instructions until al dente.

- Drain the pasta, reserving a little of the cooking water, and return to the pan. Stir through the cheeses, adding a little cooking water to loosen. Season well.

- Spoon on to serving plates and serve topped with the tomato salsa and basil leaves.

---

2 Fettuccine with Goats' Cheese and Roasted Tomatoes Place 200 g (7 oz) cherry tomatoes in a roasting tin and drizzle over a little olive oil. Place in a preheated oven, 180°C (350°F), Gas Mark 4, for 15 minutes or until cooked through. Sprinkle over a handful of chopped oregano leaves, a pinch of sugar and 1 tablespoon balsamic vinegar 2 minutes before the end of the cooking time. Meanwhile, cook and drain the fettuccine as above, reserving a little of the cooking water. Stir through 125 g (4 oz) soft goats' cheese, 5 tablespoons mascarpone cheese and a handful of grated Parmesan cheese, adding a little cooking water to loosen. Spoon into bowls and serve topped with the roasted tomatoes and a few toasted pine nuts.

3 Goats' Cheese Pasta Bake with Tomato Salsa Cook 400 g (13 oz) penne according to the pack instructions until al dente. Meanwhile, mix together the goats' and cream cheeses with 50 g (2 oz) low-fat crème fraîche in a bowl. Thin with a little milk to make a sauce, then toss together with the drained pasta. Spoon into an ovenproof dish, top with a handful of grated Parmesan cheese, if liked, and bake in a preheated oven, 190°C (375°F), Gas Mark 5, for 15–20 minutes or until bubbling and cooked through. Meanwhile, make the tomato salsa as above. Top the pasta with the salsa and serve immediately.

Open Butternut Squash and Ricotta Lasagne

Serves 4

1 red onion, sliced
½ butternut squash, peeled, deseeded and sliced
1 tablespoon olive oil
6 dried lasagne sheets
250 g (8 oz) ricotta cheese
75 g (3 oz) mascarpone cheese
juice and grated rind of ½ lemon, plus extra rind to garnish
50 g (2 oz) rocket leaves
salt

- Place the onion and butternut squash in a roasting tin and drizzle with the oil. Bake in a preheated oven, 220°C (425°F), Gas Mark 7, for 15 minutes or until golden and softened.

- Meanwhile, cook the lasagne sheets in a large saucepan of boiling salted water for 7–10 minutes or until soft, then cut each sheet in half. While the pasta is cooking, mix together the ricotta, mascarpone and lemon juice and rind in a small bowl.

- Place 1 half-sheet of lasagne on each of 4 serving plates, top with some squash and onion, then add some of the ricotta mixture. Repeat the layers until all the pasta is used up. Scatter over the rocket and lemon rind and serve immediately.

10 Speedy Butternut Squash and Ricotta Pasta Cook the squash, prepared as above and cut into cubes, and 400 g (13 oz) penne in a saucepan of boiling water for 10 minutes. Drain, reserving a little of the cooking water, and return to the pan. Stir through 1 tablespoon mascarpone cheese, adding a little cooking water to loosen, then dollop over 250 g (8 oz) ricotta cheese. Serve immediately.

30 Butternut Squash and Ricotta Cannelloni Cook the squash, prepared as above, in a saucepan of boiling salted water for 10 minutes until soft, then drain well. Place in a food processor or blender and blend to a purée. Mix together with the ricotta and mascarpone cheeses as above. Spoon over 8 fresh lasagne sheets and roll up. Place in an ovenproof dish and pour over 350 ml (12 fl oz) shop-bought tomato pasta sauce and top with 125 g (4 oz) grated mozzarella cheese. Place in a preheated oven, 200°C (400°F), Gas Mark 6, for 15 minutes or until golden and cooked through.

Pasta Niçoise

Serves 4

400 g (13 oz) ditalini
150 g (5 oz) green beans, trimmed
200 g (7 oz) can tuna in spring
   water, drained and flaked
100 g (3½ oz) cherry tomatoes,
   quartered
50 g (2 oz) pitted black olives
   (preferably Niçoise)
75 g (3 oz) rocket leaves
salt

For the dressing

3 anchovy fillets in oil, drained
   and chopped
1 garlic clove, crushed
2 teaspoons white wine vinegar
2 tablespoons extra virgin olive oil

- Cook the pasta in a large saucepan of salted boiling water according to the pack instructions until al dente. Add the beans 5 minutes before the end of the cooking time and cook until just tender.

- Meanwhile, make the dressing. Mash together the anchovies and garlic in a bowl, then mix in the vinegar and oil.

- Drain the pasta and beans, reserving a little of the cooking water, and return to the pan. Stir through the dressing, adding a little cooking water to loosen if needed. Mix through the remaining ingredients and serve immediately.

---

2 **Pasta Niçoise with Griddled Fiery Tuna** Make the recipe as above, omitting the canned tuna. Meanwhile, rub 1 tablespoon olive oil and a pinch of dried chilli flakes over 4 tuna steaks and season well. Heat a griddle pan until smoking, add the tuna steaks and cook for 3–5 minutes on each side, until browned on the outside but still rare inside. Slice the griddled tuna and add to the pasta.

---

3 **Pasta Niçoise with Red Pepper and Tomato Sauce** Place 200 g (7 oz) halved tomatoes and 1 halved, cored and deseeded red pepper in a roasting tin and drizzle with olive oil. Place in a preheated oven, 200°C (400°F), Gas Mark 6, for 20–25 minutes or until soft and lightly charred. Place in a food processor or blender with the tomatoes and pulse together to form a chunky sauce. Meanwhile, make the recipe as above. Drizzle the sauce on top of the pasta to serve.

Spaghetti with Kale and Gruyère

10

Serves 4

400 g (13 oz) wholewheat spaghetti

200 g (7 oz) kale, chopped

2 tablespoons olive oil

2 garlic cloves, sliced

1 tablespoon white wine vinegar

salt and pepper

25 g (1 oz) Gruyère cheese, shaved, to serve

- Cook the pasta in a large saucepan of salted boiling water according to the pack instructions until al dente. Add the kale 5 minutes before the end of the cooking time and cook until tender.

- Meanwhile, heat the oil in a frying pan, add the garlic and cook for 30 seconds until beginning to turn golden. Add the vinegar and cook for a further couple of seconds. Remove from the heat.

- Drain the pasta and kale and return to the pan. Stir through the garlic oil and season.

- Spoon into serving bowls and serve topped with shavings of Gruyère.

20 **Spaghetti with Slow-Cooked Kale and Gruyère** Heat a little olive oil in a large saucepan, add 1 sliced onion and cook until softened. Add 1 chopped garlic clove and 200 g (7 oz) chopped kale and cook for a further 3 minutes, then reduce the heat and pour over 2 tablespoons water. Cover with a lid and cook for 15 minutes, adding more water if needed until the kale is wilted and soft. Meanwhile, cook and drain the wholewheat spaghetti as above. Toss through the kale and 2 chopped tomatoes and serve topped with Gruyère shavings as above.

30 **Kale and Butternut Squash Spaghetti with Gruyère** Toss ½ peeled, deseeded and cubed butternut squash with 2 tablespoons olive oil in a roasting tin. Place in a preheated oven, 200°C (400°F), Gas Mark 6, for 20 minutes or until soft and golden. Meanwhile, cook and drain the wholewheat spaghetti and kale as above. Pour 350 ml (12 fl oz) shop-bought tomato pasta sauce into a saucepan and heat through, then toss through the pasta with the kale and cooked squash. Serve topped with Gruyère shavings as above.

Mushroom Tagliatelle Bolognese

Serves 4

300 g (10 oz) mixed mushrooms, trimmed

2 tablespoons olive oil, plus extra to serve (optional)

1 onion, finely chopped

1 garlic clove, crushed

handful of thyme leaves

100 ml (3½ fl oz) dry white wine

1 teaspoon tomato purée

300 ml (½ pint) passata

400 g (13 oz) tagliatelle

salt and pepper

grated Parmesan cheese, to serve

- Using a sharp knife, finely chop the mushrooms until they resemble breadcrumbs. Alternatively, whizz the mushrooms in a food processor, being careful not to over-process them so that they become mushy.

- Heat the oil in a large frying pan, add the onion, mushrooms, garlic and thyme and cook over a medium heat for 5 minutes, stirring frequently, until softened. Pour over the wine and cook for 5 minutes or until all the wine has been absorbed. Stir in the tomato purée and passata and simmer for a further 10 minutes. Season to taste.

- Meanwhile, cook the pasta in a large saucepan of salted boiling water according to the pack instructions until al dente. Drain and return to the pan, then toss in a little olive oil, if liked, and stir through the sauce.

- Spoon into serving bowls and serve scattered with the Parmesan.

Easy Mushroom Tagliatelle Heat a little olive oil in a frying pan, add 2 chopped garlic cloves and cook for 1 minute until softened. Add 250 g (8 oz) trimmed and sliced mushrooms and a pinch of dried chilli flakes and cook for a further couple of minutes until softened. Meanwhile, cook and drain the tagliatelle as above. Toss the mushrooms, 3 chopped tomatoes and a handful of chopped basil leaves through the drained pasta and serve immediately.

Wild Mushroom Tagliatelle with Porcini Sauce Soak 25 g (1 oz) dried porcini mushrooms in 50 ml (2 fl oz) boiling water for 15 minutes until softened. Meanwhile, heat a little olive oil in a frying pan, add 1 chopped onion and 1 chopped garlic clove and fry gently until very soft. Stir in 1 teaspoon tomato purée, then pour over 100 ml (3½ fl oz) dry white wine and bubble for a couple of minutes until reduced by half. Pour in the porcini mushrooms with their soaking liquid and 50 g (2 oz) crème fraîche. Fry 150 g (5 oz) mixed wild mushrooms, trimmed and halved if large, in a little olive oil until soft. While the mushrooms are frying, cook and drain the tagliatelle as above. Toss through the wild mushrooms and mushroom sauce and serve as above.

10 Conchiglie with Spinach and Goats' Cheese

Serves 4

1 tablespoon olive oil
1 garlic clove, finely chopped
250 g (8 oz) baby spinach leaves, chopped
handful of mint leaves, chopped
500 g (1 lb) fresh conchiglie
100 g (3½ oz) soft goats' cheese
25 g (1 oz) roughly chopped walnuts
salt and pepper

- Heat the oil in a large saucepan, add the garlic and cook for 30 seconds until beginning to turn golden. Add the spinach and cover with a lid. Cook for a couple of minutes or until the spinach has wilted, then stir through the mint.

- Meanwhile, cook the pasta in a large saucepan of salted boiling water according to the pack instructions until al dente. Drain, reserving a little of the cooking water, and return to the pan. Stir through the spinach mixture, adding a little cooking water to loosen if needed, and season.

- Spoon into serving bowls, crumble over the goats' cheese and scatter over the walnuts. Serve immediately.

---

2 **Spinach, Courgette and Olive Conchiglie with Goats' Cheese** Cook 400 g (13 oz) dried conchiglie according to the pack instructions until al dente. Meanwhile, cook the garlic, spinach and mint as above. Slice 100 g (3½ oz) baby courgettes in half. Heat 1 tablespoon olive oil in a frying pan, add the courgettes and cook for a couple of minutes. Turn over, add a handful of pitted black olives to the pan and cook for a further 2 minutes until golden all over. Drain the pasta, reserving a little of the cooking water, and return to the pan. Toss through the courgette mixture and spinach, adding a little cooking water to loosen if needed. Serve with goats' cheese as above.

3 **Spinach, Ham and Goats' Cheese Pasta Bake** Cook 400 g (13 oz) dried conchiglie according to the pack instructions until al dente, adding 250 g (8 oz) baby spinach leaves just before draining. Meanwhile, melt 25 g (1 oz) butter in a saucepan and stir in 25 g (1 oz) plain flour to make a smooth paste. Cook until golden, then gradually whisk in 300 ml (½ pint) milk. Bring to the boil and simmer until slightly thickened, stirring often, then stir through 50 g (2 oz) soft goats' cheese. Drain the pasta and spinach and stir into the sauce with 4 slices of ham, cut into bite-sized pieces. Pour into an ovenproof dish, crumble over a further 50 g (2 oz) goats' cheese and a handful of fresh white breadcrumbs. Place in a preheated oven, 200°C (400°F), Gas Mark 6, for 15 minutes or until heated through and bubbling.

PAS-HEAL-JUA

20 Fusilli with Lentils, Kale and Caramelized Onion

Serves 4

2 tablespoons olive oil
2 onions, cut into rings
pinch of dried chilli flakes
2 garlic cloves, finely sliced
50 g (2 oz) Puy lentils, rinsed
and drained
400 g (13 oz) tricolore fusilli
125 g (4 oz) kale, chopped
salt and pepper

- Heat the oil in a nonstick frying pan, add the onions and chilli flakes, season well and cook over a low heat for 15 minutes or until very soft and lightly browned. Add the garlic and cook for a further couple of minutes.

- Meanwhile, cook the lentils in a saucepan of simmering water according to the pack instructions, then drain.

- While the onions and lentils are cooking, cook the pasta in a large saucepan of salted boiling water according to the pack instructions until al dente. Add the kale 3 minutes before the end of the cooking time and cook until tender. Drain, reserving a little of the cooking water, and return to the pan. Toss together with the lentils, adding a little cooking water to loosen if needed.

- Spoon into serving bowls and serve scattered with the caramelized onions.

10 Easy Lentil, Caramelized Onion and Tomato Fusilli

Place a 250 g (8 oz) pouch ready-cooked Puy lentils in a saucepan and stir in 6 tablespoons shop-bought fresh sun-dried tomato pesto and 2 tablespoons shop-bought ready-cooked fried onion. Add 1 chopped tomato and a little water to make a sauce, then heat through. Meanwhile, cook and drain the fusilli as above. Stir through the sauce and serve topped with extra ready-cooked fried onion.

30 Fusilli with Roasted Shallots and Lentils

Place 200 g (7 oz) peeled shallots in a roasting tin and toss with 2 tablespoons olive oil. Place in a preheated oven, 190°C (375°F), Gas Mark 5, for 20–25 minutes or until golden and soft. Drizzle over 1 tablespoon balsamic vinegar and 1 teaspoon sugar and bake for a further 2 minutes. Meanwhile, cook and drain the lentils and fusilli as above, then toss together with the shallots. Serve drizzled with a little more balsamic vinegar and topped with 25 g (1 oz) crumbled feta cheese.

Sicilian Cauliflower and Anchovy Rigatoni

Serves 2

200 g (7 oz) rigatoni
½ small cauliflower, broken
   into florets
1 tablespoon olive oil
4 anchovy fillets in oil, drained
   and finely chopped
2 garlic cloves, sliced
1 red chilli, deseeded if liked,
   and sliced
25 g (1 oz) raisins
25 g (1 oz) toasted pine nuts
juice and grated rind of ½ lemon
salt
chopped flat-leaf parsley,
   to garnish

- Cook the pasta in a large saucepan of salted boiling water according to the pack instructions until al dente.

- Meanwhile, cook the cauliflower in a saucepan of boiling water for 5 minutes, then drain. Heat the oil in a small frying pan, add the anchovies, garlic and chilli and cook for a couple of minutes until sizzling. Add the cauliflower and cook for a further couple of minutes until beginning to turn golden. Stir in the raisins and pine nuts, then add the lemon juice.

- Drain the pasta, reserving a little of the cooking water, and return to the pan. Stir through the cauliflower mixture, adding a little cooking water to loosen if needed.

- Spoon into serving bowls and serve sprinkled with the lemon rind and parsley.

---

10 **Easy Cauliflower Tagliarelle with Anchovy Butter** Cook 200 g (7 oz) tagliarelle according to the pack instructions until al dente, adding the cauliflower, prepared as above, for 7 minutes of the cooking time. Meanwhile, mash the grated rind of ½ lemon and 4 drained anchovy fillets into 25 g (1 oz) softened butter in a bowl. Drain the pasta and cauliflower and spoon into serving bowls. Serve with the anchovy butter dabbed over.

30 **Rigatoni with Roasted Cauliflower in Anchovy Oil** Mash together 2 garlic cloves, 5 drained anchovy fillets and 1 tablespoon oil in a bowl. Place the cauliflower, prepared as above, in a roasting tin and toss in the oil. Place in a preheated oven, 200°C (400°F), Gas Mark 6, for 20–25 minutes or until soft and lightly charred. Meanwhile, cook and drain the rigatoni as above. Toss the cauliflower with 1 drained and chopped roasted red pepper from a jar and stir through the pasta with a squeeze of lemon juice. Serve immediately.

Spiced Lentils with Vermicelli

Serves 4

125 g (4 oz) green or brown
  lentils, rinsed and drained
3 tablespoons olive oil
75 g (3 oz) vermicelli
200 g (7 oz) long-grain rice
400 ml (14 fl oz) hot chicken
  stock
2 large onions, thinly sliced
3 garlic cloves, crushed
¼ teaspoon dried chilli flakes
1 teaspoon ground cumin
400 ml (14 fl oz) passata
salt and pepper
chopped coriander leaves,
  to garnish

- Cook the lentils in a saucepan of simmering water for 25 minutes or according to the pack instructions, then drain.

- Meanwhile, heat 1 tablespoon of the oil in a saucepan. Break the vermicelli into small strips about 2 cm (¾ inch) long. Add to the pan and cook for a couple of minutes until beginning to colour. Add the rice, stir and then pour over the stock.

- Bring to the boil, then reduce the heat and simmer for about 10 minutes or until the stock has nearly boiled away. Reduce the heat to its lowest setting, cover with a lid and leave for 5 minutes or until the rice is cooked through.

- While the lentils and rice are cooking, heat the remaining oil in a frying pan, add the onions and cook for 20 minutes or until lightly browned, stirring frequently. Add the garlic, chilli flakes and cumin and cook for a further 1 minute. Remove some of the onions and set aside for garnish. Pour the passata into the pan, season well and simmer until ready to serve.

- Carefully stir the lentils through the rice, then spoon into serving bowls. Pour over the spicy tomato sauce and top with the reserved onions, the coriander and serve.

---

1 **Lentil Pasta Salad**
Cook 300 g (10 oz) orzo according to the pack instructions. Add 125 g (4 oz) frozen broad beans to the pan 3–4 minutes before the end of the cooking time and cook until tender. Drain, then cool under cold running water and drain again. Drain and rinse 200 g (7 oz) canned lentils. Mix with the pasta in a dish with 1 finely chopped shallot, the juice of 1 lemon and a handful of chopped basil leaves.

2 **Lentil Spaghetti Bolognese**
Cook 400 g (13 oz) wholewheat spaghetti according to the pack instructions until al dente. Meanwhile, heat 1 tablespoon olive oil in a large frying pan, add 2 sliced garlic cloves and cook for 1 minute. Pour over 400 ml (14 fl oz) passata and simmer for 10 minutes. Stir in a rinsed and drained 400 g (13 oz) can lentils and heat through. Drain the pasta and return to the pan.

Mix together with the lentil sauce and serve scattered with grated Parmesan cheese, if liked.

Pasta with Courgettes, Peas, Tomatoes and Feta

Serves 4

2 courgettes
1 tablespoon olive oil
400 g (13 oz) tagliarelle pasta
125 g (4 oz) frozen peas
50 g (2 oz) feta cheese
125 g (4 oz) cherry tomatoes, halved
salt and pepper
basil leaves, to garnish

- Using a vegetable peeler, thinly slice the courgettes, then rub over the oil and season well. Heat a griddle pan until smoking, then add the courgettes and cook for about 2 minutes. Turn over and cook for a further 2 minutes until just soft and lightly charred. Set aside.

- Cook the pasta in a large saucepan of salted boiling water according to the pack instructions until al dente. Add the peas 2 minutes before the end of the cooking time and cook until tender. Drain, reserving a little of the cooking water, and return to the pan.

- Mash half the feta with 2 tablespoons of the cooking water and stir through the pasta, adding more cooking water to loosen if needed. Toss together with the tomatoes and courgettes. Crumble over the remaining feta and serve sprinkled with basil leaves.

10 Quick Courgette, Pea, Tomato and Feta Pasta Cook the tagliarelle pasta and peas as above. Meanwhile, mash together 50 g (2 oz) feta cheese, 2 tablespoons milk, a handful of chopped mint leaves and 4 drained and finely chopped sun-dried tomatoes in oil in a bowl, then finely grate in 2 courgettes. Drain the pasta and peas, then toss through the courgette mixture. Serve immediately.

30 Courgette, Tomato and Feta Pasta Bake with Pea Shoots Cook 400 g (13 oz) fusilli according to pack instructions until al dente. Drain and return to the pan, then mix through a 400 g (13 oz) can chopped tomatoes. Meanwhile, cook the courgettes as above and then stir into the pasta with a handful of chopped basil leaves. Pour into an ovenproof dish, scatter over a handful of dried white breadcrumbs and 75 g (3 oz) crumbled feta cheese. Place in a preheated oven, 190°C (375°F), Gas Mark 5, for 15 minutes or until golden and cooked through. Serve topped with pea shoot leaves mixed with a little lemon juice and extra virgin olive oil.

Spaghetti with Mini Tuna Balls

Serves 4

2 spring onions, thinly sliced
2 x 185 g (6½ oz) cans tuna in
   spring water, drained
1 egg yolk, lightly beaten
50 g (2 oz) fresh white
   breadcrumbs
handful of mint leaves, chopped,
   plus extra to garnish (optional)
pinch of dried chilli flakes
1 tablespoon olive oil
375 ml (13 fl oz) shop-bought
   tomato pasta sauce
400 g (13 oz) spaghetti
salt and pepper

- Mix together the spring onions, tuna, egg yolk, bread-crumbs, mint and chilli flakes in a bowl and season. Lightly wet your hands, then shape the mixture into small balls, each about the size of a walnut. The mixture should make about 12 balls.

- Heat the oil in a nonstick frying pan and cook the tuna balls for 5–10 minutes or until golden all over and cooked through. Pour over the tomato pasta sauce and cook for a further 5 minutes until the sauce is heated through, adding a little extra water if the sauce becomes too thick.

- Meanwhile, cook the pasta in a large saucepan of salted boiling water according to the pack instructions until al dente. Drain and stir through the sauce.

- Spoon into serving bowls and serve sprinkled with extra chopped mint, if liked.

10 Simple Tuna Spaghetti Cook and drain the spaghetti as above. Meanwhile, toss together a drained 120 g (4 oz) can tuna in spring water, 1 chopped red chilli, deseeded if liked, 150 g (5 oz) halved cherry tomatoes and a good squeeze of lemon juice in a bowl. Stir through the drained pasta with a large handful of rocket leaves. Serve immediately.

30 Spaghetti with Spiced Fresh Tuna Balls Chop a 400G (13 oz) piece of fresh tuna on a chopping board as finely as you can. Make the mini tuna balls as above, replacing the canned tuna with the fresh tuna and adding 1 teaspoon ground cumin and 15 g (½ oz) raisins. Continue with the recipe as above.

Pasta Primavera

Serves 4

400 g (13 oz) farfalle
1 tablespoon olive oil
4 spring onions, sliced
25 ml (1 fl oz) dry white wine
150 g (5 oz) asparagus tips
125 g (4 oz) frozen broad beans
50 g (2 oz) low-fat cream cheese
salt and pepper
chopped chives, to garnish
 (optional)

- Cook the pasta in a large saucepan of salted boiling water according to the pack instructions until al dente.

- Meanwhile, heat the oil in a frying pan with a lid, add the spring onions and cook for 1–2 minutes until softened. Pour over the wine and bubble for a couple of minutes until syrupy. Add the asparagus and 50 ml (2 fl oz) of water, then cover with the lid and simmer for 5 minutes.

- Add the broad beans to the pan, followed by the cream cheese. Stir around, adding more water if needed until the cream cheese melts into the sauce and the broad beans are tender.

- Drain the pasta, reserving a little of the cooking water, and return to the pan. Stir through the vegetable sauce, adding a little cooking water to loosen if needed.

- Spoon into serving bowls and serve sprinkled with chives.

---

10 Speedy Pasta Primavera Cook 400 g (13 oz) spaghettini according to pack instructions until al dente. Add the asparagus and broad beans to the pan 3 minutes before the end of the cooking time and cook until tender. Meanwhile, mix together the cream cheese with 2–3 tablespoons shop-bought fresh green pesto in a bowl. Drain the pasta and vegetables, reserving a little of the cooking water, and return to the pan. Stir the cream cheese mixture into the pasta, adding a little cooking water to loosen, and serve immediately.

30 Pasta Primavera with Griddled Vegetables Heat a griddle pan until smoking hot. Toss 4 sliced spring onions, 150 g (5 oz) asparagus tips and 125 g (4 oz) trimmed and cleaned baby leeks with olive oil in a bowl, then place half the vegetables in the hot griddle pan and cook for 7–10 minutes or until soft and charred. Remove from the pan and keep warm, then repeat with the remaining vegetables. Meanwhile, cook and drain the farfalle as above. Toss through the griddled vegetables with a good squeeze of lemon juice, a little cooking water and a big handful of grated Parmesan cheese. Chop together the rind of ½ lemon, 1 garlic clove and 1 tablespoon flat-leaf parsley. Serve scattered over the pasta.

Penne with Caponata Sauce

Serves 4

1 aubergine, cubed

4 tablespoons olive oil

1 onion, sliced

1 garlic clove, sliced

2 celery sticks, sliced

75 g (3 oz) large pitted
   green olives

1 tablespoon capers, rinsed
   and drained

50 ml (2 fl oz) white wine vinegar

2 tablespoons sugar

400 g (13 oz) can cherry
   tomatoes

400 g (13 oz) penne

salt and pepper

torn basil leaves, to garnish

- Toss the aubergine in 2 tablespoons of the oil, place on a baking sheet and season. Place in a preheated oven, 190°C (375°F), Gas Mark 5, for 20 minutes until soft and browned.

- Meanwhile, make the caponata sauce. Heat the remaining oil in a large frying pan, add the onion and garlic and cook gently for 5 minutes. Add the celery and cook for a further 5 minutes until very soft. Stir in the olives and capers, followed by the vinegar, sugar and tomatoes. Bring to the boil, then reduce the heat and simmer for 15 minutes, adding the baked aubergine to heat through for a couple of minutes. Season to taste.

- While the aubergine and sauce are cooking, cook the pasta in a large saucepan of salted boiling water according to the pack instructions until al dente. Drain, reserving a little of the cooking water, and return to the pan. Toss through the sauce, adding a little cooking water to loosen if needed.

- Spoon into serving bowls and serve sprinkled with the basil.

1 Quick Aubergine and Tomato Pasta

Cut 1 aubergine into thin slices, rub with olive oil and season well. Cook under a preheated hot grill for 3–5 minutes on each side. Meanwhile, cook the penne as above. Mix together 1 tablespoon balsamic vinegar, ½ teaspoon sugar and 3 tablespoons extra-virgin olive oil in a bowl and season. Drain the pasta and return to the pan. Mix together with the aubergine, 150 g (5 oz) halved cherry tomatoes and the dressing. Serve immediately.

2 Penne with Aubergine

Caponata Sauce Make the caponata sauce as above, omitting the celery. Meanwhile, rub oil on to thin slices of aubergine, season and cook under a preheated hot grill for 3 minutes on each side. Add to the sauce with a 2 teaspoons grated plain dark chocolate to enrich the sauce and heat through. While the sauce is cooking, cook and drain the penne as above. Stir through the sauce and serve immediately.

PAS-HEAL-DYE

Roast Chicken, Tomato and Feta Pasta

Serves 4

2 tablespoons olive oil
2 boneless, skinless
 chicken breasts
1 teaspoon honey
juice of 1 lemon
200 g (7 oz) cherry tomatoes
400 g (13 oz) ruote pasta
handful of oregano leaves,
 chopped
25 g (1 oz) feta cheese
salt and pepper

- Brush a little of the oil over each chicken breast, then place on a baking sheet and season well. Place in a preheated oven, 200°C (400°F), Gas Mark 6, for 12 minutes or until nearly cooked through.

- Drizzle over the honey and a good squeeze of the lemon juice and scatter the tomatoes around. Return to the oven and cook for a further 5 minutes or until the chicken is cooked through.

- Meanwhile, cook the pasta in a large saucepan of salted boiling water according to the pack instructions until al dente. Drain, reserving a little of the cooking water, and return to the pan. Stir through lemon juice to taste, the remaining oil and the oregano.

- Cut the chicken into bite-sized pieces and stir through the pasta with the tomatoes, adding a little cooking water if needed. Spoon into serving bowls, crumble over the feta cheese and serve immediately.

1 Simple Chicken, Tomato and Feta Tagliarelle Cook and drain 400 g (13 oz) tagliarelle according to the pack instructions until al dente. Toss through 2 shop-bought roasted chicken breasts, skin discarded and flesh torn into shreds, a large handful of drained sunblush tomatoes in oil and a little balsamic vinegar to taste. Serve sprinkled with basil leaves and the feta as above.

3 Tomato and Feta Pasta with Griddled Chicken Mix together 1 crushed garlic clove, a handful of oregano leaves, the juice of ½ lemon and 3 tablespoons extra virgin olive oil in a bowl, then add 2 boneless, skinless chicken breasts and marinate for 15 minutes. Heat a griddle pan until smoking, then add the chicken and cook for 5–7 minutes on each side or until just cooked through. Drizzle a little olive oil over 200 g (7 oz) cherry tomatoes on a baking sheet and cook under a preheated hot grill for 1–2 minutes until lightly coloured. Meanwhile, cook and drain the ruote pasta as above. Mash 50 g (2 oz) feta cheese with 3 tablespoons creme fraiche in a bowl and toss through the drained pasta with the tomatoes. Cut the chicken into slices and serve on top of the pasta with extra feta crumbled over, if liked.

Red Pepper and Walnut Spaghetti

Serves 4

2 tablespoons olive oil

2 red peppers

1 shallot, finely chopped

1 garlic clove, finely chopped

75 g (3 oz) walnuts

1 tablespoon pomegranate molasses or balsamic vinegar to taste

4 tablespoons low-fat cream cheese

400 g (13 oz) spaghetti

handful of chopped flat-leaf parsley

salt and pepper

- Rub 1 tablespoon of the olive oil over the red peppers. Cook under a preheated hot grill for 10 minutes, turning frequently, until charred all over. Place in a plastic food bag, seal and leave for 5 minutes. When cool, peel away the blackened skin. Cut in half, remove the seeds and slice.

- Meanwhile, heat the remaining oil in a small frying pan, add the shallot and garlic and cook for 3–5 minutes until softened. Dry-fry the walnuts in a separate frying pan, shaking frequently, for 3 minutes or until lightly toasted. Add the shallot mixture and most of the walnuts, reserving a few, to a food processor or blender with the pomegranate molasses or balsamic vinegar and whizz together to form a thick paste. Stir in the cream cheese and season well.

- Cook the pasta in a large pan of salted boiling water according to pack instructions until al dente. Drain, reserving a couple of tablespoons of the cooking water, and return to the pan. Toss through the nut paste, adding cooking water to loosen. Stir in the peppers and parsley. Pile on to serving bowls and serve sprinkled with the reserved chopped nuts.

1 **Spaghetti with Quick Red Pepper and Walnut Sauce** Cook and drain the spaghetti as above. Meanwhile, place the walnuts, garlic and cream cheese as above with 2 drained roasted red peppers from a jar and a handful of chopped basil leaves in a small food processor or blender and whizz together to form a sauce. Toss through the drained pasta and serve topped with extra chopped walnuts, if liked.

3 **Red Pepper and Walnut Spaghetti with Mussels** Grill and skin the red peppers as above, then finely chop. Meanwhile, heat a little olive oil in a large saucepan, add 1 chopped shallot and 2 chopped garlic cloves and cook until softened. Pour over 100 ml (3½ fl oz) dry white wine and 100 ml (3½ fl oz) hot fish stock and cook for 10 minutes until reduced down. Add 450 g (14½ oz) debearded and cleaned mussels, cover with a lid and cook for 5 minutes until the mussels have opened. Discard any that remain closed. Remove the mussels from the pan. While the peppers and sauce are cooking, cook and drain the spaghetti as above. Chop 75 g (3 oz) walnuts and add to the pan with 4 tablespoons low-fat cream cheese and the red peppers. Stir to make a sauce, then return the mussels to the pan with the drained pasta and toss together. Serve sprinkled with chopped flat-leaf parsley.

Pasta with Seafood and Roasted Butternut Squash

Serves 4

400 g (13 oz) butternut squash, peeled, deseeded and cubed

2 tablespoons olive oil

400 g (13 oz) tripoline pasta

1 onion, finely chopped

2 garlic cloves, finely chopped

1 red chilli, deseeded if liked, and finely chopped

75 ml (3 fl oz) dry white wine

500 g (1 lb) mussels, debearded and cleaned

salt and pepper

chopped coriander leaves, to garnish

- Toss the butternut squash in 1 tablespoon of the oil in a roasting tin and season well. Place in a preheated oven, 200°C (400°F), Gas Mark 6, for 15 minutes. Turn over and cook for a further 10 minutes or until soft and lightly browned.

- Meanwhile, cook the pasta in a large saucepan of salted boiling water according to the pack instructions until al dente.

- Heat the remaining oil in another large saucepan, add the onion, garlic and chilli and cook for a couple of minutes until softened. Pour over the wine and bring to the boil. Reduce the heat and simmer for 1–2 minutes. Add the mussels, cover with a lid and cook for 5 minutes until the mussels have opened. Discard any that remain closed.

- Drain the pasta and return to the pan. Stir in the butternut squash and mussels with all the cooking juices. Season well.

- Spoon into serving bowls and serve sprinkled with the coriander.

1 **Easy Butternut Squash and Seafood Tripoline** Cook 400 g (13 oz) penne and the butternut squash, prepared as above, in a large saucepan of boiling water for 10 minutes until soft. Drain, return to the pan and toss together with 200 g (7 oz) shop-bought ready-cooked mussels, a good squeeze of lemon juice and some dried chilli flakes. Serve as above.

2 **Pasta with Butternut Squash and Seafood Sauce** Heat a little olive oil in a large frying pan, add the butternut squash, prepared as above, and cook over a low heat for 12–15 minutes or until soft. Place in a food processor or blender and whizz to form a purée. Heat a little olive oil in a frying pan, add 1 finely chopped onion and cook until softened, then add the squash, 75 g (3 oz) half-fat crème fraîche and enough water to make a sauce. Add 200 g (7 oz) large cooked peeled prawns and cook for 3 minutes or until heated through. Meanwhile, cook and drain the tripoline pasta as above. Stir through the sauce and serve sprinkled with 25 g (1 oz) soft goats' cheese and chopped flat-leaf parsley.

Gnocchi with Salmon in a Chilli Tomato Sauce

Serves 4

2 tablespoons olive oil
250 g (8 oz) piece of salmon fillet
1 onion, finely chopped
2 garlic cloves, finely chopped
1 teaspoon tomato purée
1–2 tablespoons sweet chilli sauce
400 g (13 oz) can chopped
  tomatoes
400 g (13 oz) dried gnocchi pasta
salt and pepper
basil leaves, to garnish

- Rub 1 tablespoon of the olive oil over the salmon and season well. Place on a baking sheet and cook in a preheated oven, 190°C (375°F), Gas Mark 5, for 12–15 minutes or until the fish is cooked through and flakes easily.

- Meanwhile, heat the remaining oil in a saucepan, add the onion and garlic and cook for a couple of minutes until softened. Stir in the tomato purée, then add the sweet chilli sauce and tomatoes. Bring to the boil, then reduce the heat and simmer until ready to serve.

- Cook the pasta in a large saucepan of salted boiling water according to the pack instructions until al dente. Drain, reserving a little of the cooking water, and return to the pan. Stir through the tomato sauce, adding a little cooking water if needed. Carefully flake the fish, removing any skin and bones, and add to the pasta.

- Spoon into serving bowls and serve sprinkled with basil leaves.

Quick Gnocchi with Chilli Tomatoes and Salmon Cook and drain the gnocchi as above. Meanwhile, mix together 200 g (7 oz) halved cherry tomatoes, 3 tablespoons sweet chilli sauce and a handful of chopped basil leaves in a bowl. Stir into the drained pasta with 2 hot-smoked salmon fillets torn into bite-sized pieces. Serve immediately.

Salmon, Tomato and Chilli Pasta Salad Cook 300 g (10 oz) ditalini according to the pack instructions. Drain, then cool under cold running water and drain again. Meanwhile, place a 250 g (8 oz) piece of salmon fillet in a frying pan and pour over enough dry white wine and fish stock to cover, then poach for 15 minutes or until just cooked through. Remove any skin and bones, then flake. Mix together a good squeeze of lemon juice, 1 teaspoon honey, 1 deseeded and chopped chilli and 3 tablespoons extra virgin olive oil in a bowl. Chop and deseed 3 ripe tomatoes. Using a vegetable peeler, slice ½ cucumber into thin curls. Toss everything together in a large serving dish and serve sprinkled with chopped coriander leaves.

Summer Vegetable Tortiglioni with Basil Vinaigrette

Serves 4

2 tablespoons olive oil

1 red pepper, cored, deseeded
and sliced

1 aubergine, sliced

1 courgette, sliced

150 g (5 oz) baby plum tomatoes,
halved

400 g (13 oz) tortiglioni

25 g (1 oz) toasted pine nuts,
to serve

For the basil vinaigrette

1 tablespoon white wine vinegar

½ teaspoon Dijon mustard

2 tablespoons extra virgin
olive oil

large handful of basil leaves,
finely chopped

salt and pepper

- Rub the olive oil over the red pepper, aubergine, courgette and tomatoes and season well. Heat a griddle pan until smoking, then add the vegetables and cook in batches until softened and lightly charred.

- Meanwhile, cook the pasta in a large saucepan of salted boiling water according to the pack instructions until al dente. Drain the pasta, reserving a little of the cooking water.

- To make the vinaigrette, whisk together the vinegar and mustard in a small bowl. Slowly drizzle in the oil, whisking all the time, until a smooth vinaigrette forms. Season and stir in the basil. Alternatively, make the vinaigrette in a small food processor or blender.

- Return the pasta to the pan. Stir through a little of the vinaigrette and the griddled vegetables, adding a little cooking water to loosen if needed.

- Spoon into serving bowls and drizzle over the remaining vinaigrette. Serve scattered with the pine nuts.

Easy Grilled Vegetable Penne

Cook and drain 400 g (13 oz) penne according to the pack instructions until al dente. Meanwhile, mix together 50 g (2 oz) soft goats' cheese and 3 tablespoons shop-bought fresh green pesto in a bowl. Toss 1 chopped ready-grilled aubergine, and 1 chopped ready-grilled pepper and the cheese mixture through the drained pasta. Serve immediately.

Tortiglioni with Ratatouille Sauce

Chop the vegetables into small pieces. Heat a little olive oil in a frying pan, add the vegetables and cook in batches until golden. Meanwhile, heat 2 tablespoons olive oil in a separate saucepan, add 1 finely chopped onion and 1 finely chopped garlic clove and cook until softened. Pour over 100 ml (3½ fl oz) dry white wine and cook for 5 minutes, then pour over a 400 g (13 oz) can chopped tomatoes and simmer for a further 10 minutes. Remove the pan from the heat and whizz together with a stick blender and then add the vegetables. Return to the heat and simmer for a further 10 minutes, season well and add a handful of chopped basil leaves. While the vegetable sauce is cooking, cook and drain the tortiglioni as above. Toss the vegetable sauce through the pasta and serve immediately.

Fennel, Olive and Orange Pappardelle

Serves 4

2 tablespoons olive oil
1 fennel bulb, thinly sliced
1 red onion, sliced
2 garlic cloves, sliced
1 orange
75 ml (3 fl oz) dry white wine
50 g (2 oz) pitted black olives
400 g (13 oz) pappardelle
salt
chopped basil leaves, to garnish

- Heat the oil in a medium-sized saucepan, add the fennel, onion and garlic and cook over a low heat for 10 minutes until softened. Using a sharp knife, peel off a strip of orange peel and add to the pan with the wine. Bring to the boil, then reduce the heat and add the olives. Simmer for about 10 minutes, adding a little water if needed.

- Meanwhile, cook the pasta in a large saucepan of salted boiling water according to the pack instructions until al dente. Drain, reserving a little of the cooking water. Toss through the sauce (removing the orange peel), adding a little cooking water to loosen if needed.

- Spoon into serving bowls and finely grate over a little orange rind. Serve sprinkled with the basil.

---

1 **Quick Fennel, Olive and Orange Pappardelle** Cook the pappardelle as above. Meanwhile, heat a little olive oil in a frying pan, add 1 finely chopped fennel bulb and 1 chopped garlic clove and cook for 3 minutes until golden. Pour over 50 ml (2 fl oz) vermouth and let bubble away, then squeeze in the juice of ½ orange. Drain the pasta and return to the pan, then toss through 50 g (2 oz) pitted black olives, a handful of chopped basil leaves and the fennel sauce.

3 **Grilled Swordfish with Fennel, Olive and Orange Pasta Salad** Cut 1 fennel bulb into thick strips. Brush with olive oil, then cook under a preheated hot grill for 3 minutes on each side or until lightly charred. Set aside to cool. Cook 400 g (13 oz) penne according to the pack instructions. Drain, then cool under cold running water and drain again. Brush olive oil over 4 swordfish steaks, season and cook under a preheated medium grill for 5–7 minutes on each side or until just cooked through.

Toss together the cooled pasta, fennel, 50 g (2 oz) pitted black olives, 5 chopped tomatoes, 2 tablespoons extra virgin olive oil and a little grated orange rind. Serve alongside the swordfish steaks.

30 Penne with Blackened Broccoli, Chilli and Garlic

Serves 4

1 head of broccoli
3 tablespoons olive oil
4 garlic cloves, thinly sliced
1 red chilli, deseeded if liked, and sliced
400 g (13 oz) wholewheat penne
juice and grated rind of ½ lemon
salt and pepper

- Cut the broccoli into bite-sized florets, then place on a baking sheet and drizzle over 2 tablespoons of the oil and season well. Place in a preheated oven, 190°C (375°F), Gas Mark 5, for 20 minutes or until soft and beginning to char all over.

- Add the garlic and chilli, return to the oven and cook for a further 2 minutes until they are lightly browned.

- Meanwhile, cook the pasta in a large saucepan of salted boiling water according to the pack instructions until al dente. Drain and return to the pan. Stir in the grated lemon rind and add lemon juice to taste.

- Tip in the cooked broccoli, garlic and chilli, then season. Stir through the remaining oil and serve immediately.

1 Penne and Broccoli with Chilli and Garlic Oil Cook the penne as above. Add 1 head of broccoli, broken into florets, to the pan 4–5 minutes before the end of the cooking time and cook until just tender. Meanwhile, heat 3 tablespoons olive oil in a frying pan, add the chilli, garlic and grated lemon rind as above and cook for 1–2 minutes. Drain the pasta and broccoli and return to the pan. Toss through the flavoured oil and a squeeze of lemon juice and serve immediately.

2 Penne with Griddled Garlic and Chilli Broccoli Cook and drain the penne as above. Meanwhile, cook 1 head of broccoli, broken into florets, in a saucepan of boiling water for 2 minutes. Drain well and pat dry with kitchen paper, then toss with 1 tablespoon olive oil, 1 crushed garlic clove and a pinch of dried chilli flakes. Heat a griddle pan, add the broccoli and cook for a couple of minutes until lightly browned all over. Toss together with the drained pasta and a squeeze of lemon juice. Serve immediately.

3 Sin-Free Macaroni Cheese with Tomato

Serves 4

400 g (13 oz) macaroni
2 tablespoons cornflour
500 ml (17 fl oz) milk
250 g (8 oz) silken tofu
150 g (5 oz) Cheddar
   cheese, grated
15 g (½ oz) Parmesan cheese,
   grated
1 large tomato, sliced
salt and pepper

- Cook the pasta in a large saucepan of salted boiling water according to the pack instructions until al dente.

- Meanwhile, place the cornflour in a small saucepan and whisk in 4 tablespoons of the milk until smooth. Gradually add the remaining milk, then bring to the boil and simmer until slightly thickened.

- Place the tofu in a food processor or blender and whizz until a smooth paste forms. Add in the milk mixture and process until smooth. Stir in most of the cheeses and season well.

- Drain the pasta, then stir through the tofu sauce. Spoon into an ovenproof dish and scatter over the remaining cheese, then arrange the tomato on top.

- Place in a preheated oven, 190°C (375°F), Gas Mark 5, for 15 minutes or until golden, crispy on top and cooked through.

1 Simple Cream Cheese and Tomato

Pasta Cook and drain 400 g (13 oz) chifferi pasta according to the pack instructions, reserving a little of the cooking water. Meanwhile, mix together 6 tablespoons low-fat cream cheese and a large handful of grated Parmesan cheese in a bowl. Stir through the drained pasta, adding a little cooking water to loosen if needed, and serve scattered with 2 ripe chopped tomatoes.

2 Macaroni Cheese and Tomato Gratin

Cook and drain the macaroni as above. Meanwhile, make the tofu sauce as above. Stir the sauce through the pasta with 5 drained and chopped sunblush tomatoes in oil and a handful of basil leaves. Spoon into a heatproof dish, top with a handful of fresh white breadcrumbs and a little extra Parmesan, if liked, and cook under a preheated hot grill for a couple of minutes until lightly browned.

QuickCook

Food for Friends

Recipes listed by cooking time

3⦾

2⦾

 # Light Clam and Tomato Broth

Serves 4

150 g (5 oz) tomatoes
2 tablespoons olive oil
2 garlic cloves, finely chopped
150 ml (¼ pint) dry white wine
2 litres (3½ pints) hot chicken or
    fish stock
5 sun-dried tomatoes in oil,
    drained and finely chopped
200 g (7 oz) anellini pasta
1 kg (2 lb) clams, cleaned
salt and pepper
chopped flat-leaf parsley,
    to garnish

lemon wedges and
crusty bread, to serve

- Cut a cross at the stem end of each tomato, place in a heatproof bowl and pour over boiling water to cover. Leave for 1–2 minutes, then drain and peel off the skins. Halve the tomatoes, remove the seeds and roughly chop.

- Heat the oil in a large saucepan, add the garlic and cook for 30 seconds until beginning to turn golden. Pour over the wine and cook for 5 minutes until slightly reduced. Pour over the stock and bring to the boil. Add the fresh and sun-dried tomatoes, season and simmer for 5 minutes.

- Add the pasta and clams, cover with a lid and cook for 5 minutes until the pasta has cooked through and the clams have opened. Discard any that remain closed. Season to taste.

- Ladle into serving bowls, sprinkle with the parsley and serve with lemon wedges and crusty bread.

Simple Spaghetti with Clams Heat a little olive oil in a large saucepan, add 1 finely chopped garlic clove and 1 chopped red chilli and cook for 1 minute until softened. Pour over 75 ml (3 fl oz) dry white wine and add the cleaned clams as above. Cover and cook for 5 minutes until the clams have opened. Discard any that stay closed. Meanwhile, cook 400 g (13 oz) spaghetti according to the pack instructions until al dente. Drain and return to the pan. Toss through the clams and their cooking liquid, 3 tablespoons crème fraîche and a handful of chopped flat-leaf parsley.

Linguine with Barbecued Clams Heat a little olive oil in a frying pan, add 1 finely sliced shallot and 1 chopped red chilli, deseeded if liked, and cook for a couple of minutes until softened. Pour over 75 ml (3 fl oz) dry white wine and a pinch of saffron threads. Simmer for 5 minutes until reduced down. Pour over 200 ml (7 fl oz) shop-bought clam juice and simmer for a further 10 minutes until reduced down. Place the cleaned clams as above on the grill rack of a barbecue. Cook for 5–7 minutes, transfer to a baking sheet as they open and top with a little garlic butter. Discard any clams that remain closed. Cook for a further 5 minutes on the barbecue until the butter starts to melt. Meanwhile, cook 400 g (13 oz) linguine according to the pack instructions until al dente. Drain and toss through the sauce. Serve topped with the grilled clams.

30 Linguine with Tuna Sashimi and Rocket

Serves 2

150 g (5 oz) very fresh tuna steak
200 g (7 oz) linguine
3 tablespoons extra virgin olive
   oil, plus extra to serve
juice of ½ lemon
50 g (2 oz) rocket leaves
salt and pepper
Parmesan cheese shavings,
   to serve

- Wrap the tuna tightly in clingfilm and place in a freezer for 20 minutes and then, using a sharp knife, slice into very thin strips.

- Meanwhile, cook the pasta in a large saucepan of salted boiling water according to the pack instructions until al dente. Drain the pasta and return to the pan, then toss through the tuna with 1 tablespoon olive oil and lemon juice.

- Toss together the rocket and remaining lemon juice and 1 tablespoon oil in a bowl and season.

- Spoon the pasta into serving bowls, arrange the rocket salad on top and grind over plenty of black pepper. Serve scattered with the Parmesan shavings and drizzled with the remaining olive oil.

---

10 Wintery Tuna and Rocket Linguine

Cook the linguine as above. Meanwhile, mix together 1 egg yolk, the juice and grated rind of 1 lemon and 1 crushed garlic clove in a bowl. Drain the pasta and return to the pan. Stir through the egg mixture, 160 g (5½ oz) canned tuna, drained and flaked, a handful of rinsed and drained capers and 50 g (2 oz) rocket leaves. Serve immediately.

20 Linguine with Griddled Tuna and Rocket

Cook and drain the linguine as above. Meanwhile, rub a little olive oil over 1 large tuna steak and season well with salt and plenty of pepper. Heat a griddle pan until smoking, add the tuna and cook for 3–5 minutes on each side or until browned on the outside but still rare inside, then leave to rest for a few minutes before cutting into thick slices. Toss 50 g (2 oz)

rocket leaves in a little lemon juice and olive oil. Stir the tuna slices and rocket through the drained pasta and serve topped with Parmesan cheese shavings.

Zingy Crab Vermicelli

Serves 4

400 g (13 oz) vermicelli
250 g (8 oz) fresh white
  crabmeat
6 tablespoons crème fraîche
juice and grated rind of ½ lemon
1 red chilli, deseeded and
  finely chopped
handful of flat-leaf parsley,
  chopped
salt and pepper

- Cook the pasta in a large saucepan of salted boiling water according to the pack instructions until al dente. Drain, reserving a little of the cooking water, and return to the pan.

- Stir through the remaining ingredients, adding a little cooking water to loosen if needed, and season well. Serve immediately.

2 Crab and Proscuitto Vermicelli

Heat a little olive oil in a frying pan, add 1 finely chopped shallot and cook over a low heat until softened. Add 1 sliced garlic clove and cook for a further 1 minute, then add 150 g (5 oz) diced proscuitto and cook over a medium heat for a couple of minutes until golden. Pour over 100 ml (3½ fl oz) dry white wine and cook until reduced. Stir through the crème fraîche and crabmeat as above and heat through. Meanwhile, cook and drain the vermicelli as above, then stir through the sauce. Serve immediately.

3 Pasta with Fresh Crab

Cook the crab in 1 litre (1¾ pints) vegetable stock and 150 ml (5 fl oz) dry white wine for 15 minutes per kg. Allow the crab to cool while you cook your pasta. Cook 14 oz angel hair pasta according to the pack instructions until al dente. Pull off the claws and legs and then, with the crab's body on its back and facing away from you, bring your thumbs up under the rear edge and push firmly to lift out the core. Dig your thumb in behind the eyes and mouthparts and lift out the mass of bony and gloopy bits – the inedible parts of the digestive tract. Remove, crack open the shell, and dig out the meat inside. Meanwhile, heat a little butter in a frying pan, add 1 shallot and cook until softened.

Stir in 2 tablespoons of the brown crabmeat, then pour over 50 ml (2 fl oz) dry white wine (or the reduced poaching liquid). Simmer for a couple of minutes, then add the crème fraîche and white crabmeat as above. Drain the pasta and return to the pan. Stir through the crab sauce and serve immediately.

Pasta with Rich Mushroom Sauce and Parma Ham

Serves 6

25 g (1 oz) tablespoons butter
1 tablespoon olive oil
1 shallot, finely chopped
1 small garlic clove, crushed
75 ml (3 fl oz) dry white wine
50 ml (2 fl oz) hot chicken stock
125 ml (4 fl oz) double cream
25 g (1 oz) Parmesan cheese,
  grated, plus extra to serve
  (optional)
6 slices of Parma ham
400 g (13 oz) mixed wild
  mushrooms, trimmed and
  halved if large
625 g (1¼ lb) riccioli al barolo
  pasta
fresh basil, to garnish
salt and pepper

- Heat half of the butter and half the oil in a saucepan, add the shallot and garlic and cook for a couple of minutes until softened. Pour over the wine and bubble vigorously until syrupy and reduced down to a couple of tablespoons of liquid. Pour over the stock and cook for a further 5 minutes, then stir in the cream and Parmesan, season and keep warm.

- Heat the remaining butter and oil in a frying pan, add the Parma ham slices and cook for 1–2 minutes until they start to sizzle. Remove from the pan and set aside. Add the mushrooms to the pan and fry for 3–5 minutes or until golden and cooked through. Stir into the sauce.

- Meanwhile, cook the pasta in a large saucepan of salted boiling water according to the pack instructions until al dente. Drain the pasta, reserving a little of the cooking water. Toss through the mushroom sauce, adding a little cooking water if needed.

- Spoon into serving bowls, crumble over the Parma ham and serve scattered with extra Parmesan if liked and basil.

Mushroom and Pesto Pasta

Cook 625 g (1¼ lb) pasta as above. Meanwhile, fry the mushrooms as above in a little olive oil until softened. Drain the pasta and return to the pan. Stir through the mushrooms and 6 tablespoons shop-bought fresh green pesto. Serve topped with a handful of toasted pine nuts.

Mushroom Pasta with Slow-Cooked

Leeks Heat a little olive oil in a frying pan, add 150 g (5 oz) pancetta cubes and cook over a high heat for 5 minutes or until crispy. Reduce the heat and add 4 trimmed, cleaned and sliced leeks and 1 tablespoon chopped thyme leaves, a splash of water and cook gently for 15 minutes or until very soft and lightly caramelized. Stir through 5 tablespoons double cream and 100 g (3½ oz) Taleggio cheese, cubed, to make a sauce. Drizzle olive oil over the mushrooms, prepared as above, in a grill pan and cook under a preheated hot grill for 5 minutes or until lightly charred. Meanwhile, cook and drain the riccioli al barolo as above. Stir through the mushrooms and leek sauce and serve immediately.

2 Creamy Vodka and Tomato Tacconelli

Serves 4

15 g (½ oz) butter
8 pancetta slices
1 rosemary sprig
75 ml (3 fl oz) vodka
350 ml (12 fl oz) shop-bought
  tomato pasta sauce
400 g (13 oz) tacconelli
150 ml (¼ pint) double cream
salt and pepper
grated Parmesan cheese,
  to serve

- Heat the butter in a saucepan, add the pancetta and cook for about 3 minutes until golden and crispy. Remove from the pan and keep warm. Stir in the rosemary, then remove from the heat and pour over the vodka. Return to a high heat and cook until the vodka has reduced down to 1 tablespoon. Pour over the tomato pasta sauce, reduce the heat and simmer for 10 minutes.

- Meanwhile, cook the pasta in a large saucepan of salted boiling water according to the pack instructions until al dente.

- Remove the rosemary from the sauce, then stir in the cream. Drain the pasta, reserving a little of the cooking water, and return to the pan. Stir through the sauce, adding a little cooking water to loosen if needed, and season.

- Spoon into serving bowls, top with the pancetta slices and serve scattered with the Parmesan.

---

1 Quick Vodka and Tomato Penne

Cook 500 g (1 lb) fresh penne as above. Meanwhile, heat a little olive oil in a frying pan, add 3 tablespoons tomato purée and cook for 30 seconds. Add 100 g (3½ oz) halved baby plum tomatoes and 2 tablespoons vodka and cook for a couple of minutes until the tomatoes have softened, then stir in 150 ml (¼ pint) cream. Drain the pasta and return to the pan. Toss through the sauce and serve immediately.

3 Vodka Penne with Slow-Roasted Tomatoes

Place 150 g (5 oz) halved baby plum tomatoes in a roasting tin, drizzle over a little olive oil and season. Place in a preheated oven, 150°C (300°F), Gas Mark 2, for 20–25 minutes until lightly browned. Meanwhile, cook the penne as above. Heat 50 ml (2 fl oz) vodka in a small saucepan and bubble until reduced down to 1 tablespoon. Pour over 75 ml (3 fl oz) double cream and stir through 25 g (1 oz) grated Parmesan cheese. Drain the pasta and return to the pan. Toss through the sauce, roasted tomatoes and a handful of chopped basil leaves. Serve immediately.

Salmon and Courgette Pasta

Serves 4
150 ml (¼ pint) dry white wine
150 g (5 oz) crème fraîche
a squeeze of lemon juice
handful of dill, chopped
12 lasagne sheets
2 courgettes
4 hot-smoked salmon fillets
3 spring onions, sliced
salt and pepper

- Bring the wine to the boil in a small saucepan and boil for 5 minutes until syrupy and reduced by half. Add the crème fraîche, a squeeze of lemon juice and most of the dill. Season, then stir until mixed through.

- Meanwhile, cook the lasagne sheets in a large saucepan of salted boiling water for 3–5 minutes or until soft, then drain well. Shave the courgettes into long thin strips using a vegetable peeler.

- Cut each lasagne sheet into large irregular shapes and place in a bowl. Break the salmon into large chunks.

- Arrange the salmon and pasta on serving plates with the courgette ribbons. Drizzle over the sauce and serve sprinkled with the spring onions and the remaining dill.

---

1 Summery Courgette, Asparagus and Salmon Fettuccine Cook 400 g (13 oz) fettuccine according to the pack instructions until al dente. Add 200 g (7 oz) asparagus tips to the pan 3 minutes before the end of the cooking time and cook until just tender. Drain and return to the pan. Toss through 2 hot-smoked salmon fillets, flaked into pieces, the grated rind of 1 lemon and 100 g (3½ oz) crème fraîche. Serve topped with 1 courgette, cut into ribbons as above.

3 Courgette and Salmon Lasagne Prepare 12 fresh lasagne sheets, if necessary, according to the pack instructions. Make the wine sauce as above, then grate 2 courgettes and stir into the sauce with the flaked salmon fillets. Layer up the sauce and lasagne sheets in an ovenproof dish, finishing with a layer of lasagne. Mix together 200 g (7 oz) crème fraîche and 100 g (3½ oz) ricotta cheese in a bowl and thin with milk to make a sauce. Pour over the lasagne, sprinkle with 25 g (1 oz) grated Parmesan, then place in a preheated oven, 200°C (400°F), Gas Mark 6, for about 15 minutes or until golden and bubbling.

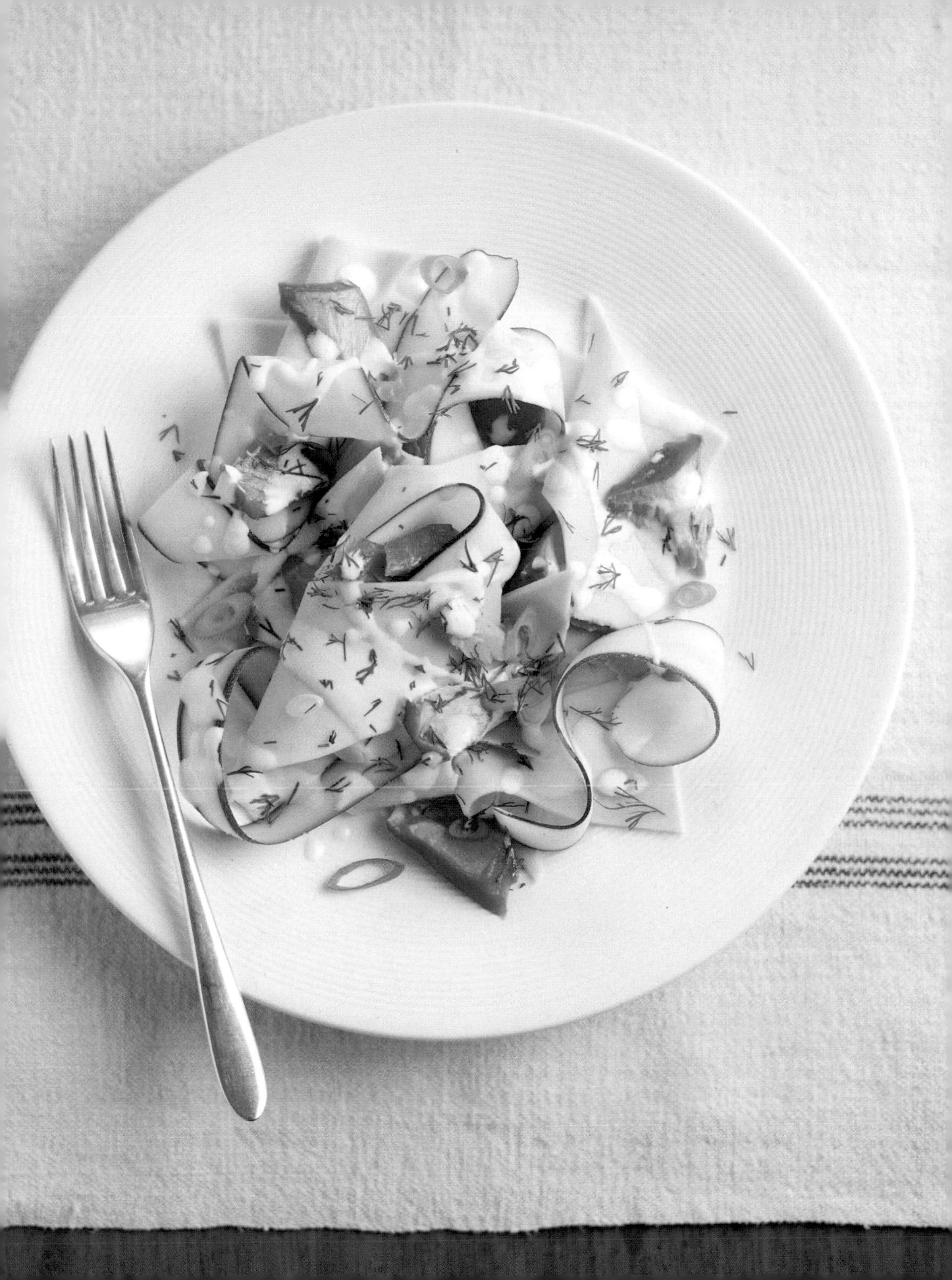

Goats' Cheese and Sun-Dried Tomato Ravioli with Basil Oil

Serves 2

1 freshly rolled large pasta sheet,
  or 24 gyoza or wonton
  wrappers
flour, for dusting
1 egg yolk, for brushing

For the filling

150 g (5 oz) soft goats' cheese
100 g (3½ oz) mascarpone
  cheese
3 sun-dried tomatoes in oil,
  drained and finely chopped
salt and pepper

For the basil oil

50 g (2 oz) basil leaves
75 ml (3 fl oz) extra virgin
  olive oil

- To make the filling, mix together the cheeses and sun-dried tomatoes in a bowl and season well.

- To make the basil oil, place the basil and oil in a small food processor or blender and whizz together, then pass through a very fine sieve to form a green oil.

- Lay the pasta sheet on a clean work surface lightly dusted with flour. Using a plain 5 cm (2 in) cutter, stamp out 24 rounds from the sheets. Place a heaped tablespoon of filling in the centre of a pasta round or wrapper and then brush a little egg around the edges. Brush the edge of a second round or wrapper and place it, moist edge down, over the filling. Gently press out any excess air and use your fingers to seal. Place on a baking sheet lightly dusted with flour. Repeat with the remaining rounds or wrappers and filling.

- Cook the pasta in a large saucepan of salted boiling water for 3 minutes or until cooked through. Remove from the pan with a slotted spoon and arrange on a serving plate. Drizzle with the oil and serve immediately.

1 **Cheese Tortelloni with Sun-Dried Tomato Pesto** Place a handful of basil leaves, 25 g (1 oz) toasted pine nuts, 5 drained sun-dried tomatoes in oil, 15 g (½ oz) grated Parmesan cheese and 3 tablespoons olive oil in a small food processor or blender and whizz to form a pesto. Cook a 250 g (8 oz) pack cheese tortelloni according to the pack instructions. Drain and return to the pan. Stir through the sun-dried tomato pesto and serve immediately.

2 **Goats' Cheese and Tomato Penne** Heat a little olive oil in a frying pan, add 1 chopped onion and cook over a low heat until softened. Stir in 1 chopped garlic clove, then pour over a 400 g (13 oz) can tomatoes and simmer for 15 minutes. Meanwhile, cook 400 g (13 oz) penne according to the pack instructions until al dente. Mash 100 g (3½ oz) soft goats' cheese in a bowl. Pour over a little of the tomato sauce and stir until the cheese melts. Add 150 g (5 oz) chopped baby spinach leaves and 75 g (3 oz) pitted black olives to the tomato sauce, followed by the warmed cheese. Drain the pasta and return to the pan, then toss through the sauce. Serve with extra cheese crumbled over, if liked.

Lamb Cutlets with Garlicky Courgette and Anchovy Tagliatelle

Serves 4

25 g (1 oz) butter
50 ml (2 fl oz) olive oil, plus
  extra for brushing
4 garlic cloves, crushed
8 anchovy fillets in oil, drained
1 rosemary sprig, leaves stripped
  and finely chopped
1 courgette, thinly sliced
8 lamb cutlets
400 g (13 oz) tagliatelle
handful of flat-leaf parsley,
  chopped
salt and pepper

- Melt the butter in a small saucepan, then add the oil and garlic and cook over a low heat for 5 minutes until softened, taking care not to burn the garlic. Add the anchovies and rosemary and cook for a couple more minutes, mashing with the back of a spoon until the anchovies melt.

- Heat a griddle pan until smoking hot. Brush the courgette slices with a little oil and cook for 3 minutes on each side until golden. Remove to a plate and keep warm. Brush the lamb cutlets with a little oil and season well. Cook for 5–7 minutes, turn over and cook for a further 5 minutes or until charred and just cooked through.

- Cook the pasta in a large pan of salted boiling water according to the pack instructions until al dente. Drain, reserving some cooking water and return to the pan. Add the garlic and anchovy oil and toss through, stirring in a little cooking water to loosen if needed, then stir in the courgette and parsley. Pile on to serving plates, arrange the lamb cutlets alongside and serve immediately.

1 **Quick Courgette and Anchovy Tagliatelle** Cook and drain the tagliatelle as above. Meanwhile, heat a little olive oil in a frying pan, add 2 chopped garlic cloves and cook for 30 seconds, then add 6 drained anchovy fillets in oil and cook for a further 2 minutes, mashing with the back of a spoon. Pour over 50 ml (2 fl oz) double cream and heat through. Finely grate 2 courgettes and stir through the drained pasta with the sauce. Serve immediately.

2 **Lamb and Red Pepper Tagliatelle with Anchovy Sauce** Cut 300 g (10 oz) lamb chops into thin strips. Heat a little olive oil in a frying pan, add the lamb and cook over a high heat until golden all over and just cooked through. Remove from the pan and set aside. Add the garlic and anchovies to the pan and cook as above. Meanwhile, cook and drain the tagliatelle as above. Slice 1 drained roasted red pepper from a jar into thin strips and stir through the drained pasta with the fried lamb and anchovy oil. Serve immediately.

PAS-FOOD-XAB

Spaghetti with Monkfish, Mussels and Fennel

Serves 4

3 tablespoons boiling water
½ teaspoon saffron threads
15 g (1½ oz) butter
1 fennel bulb, sliced
50 ml (2 fl oz) dry white wine
450 g (14½ oz) mussels,
  debearded and cleaned
150 g (5 oz) crème fraîche
1 tablespoon olive oil
300 g (10 oz) monkfish fillet,
  boned and cut into 1.5 cm
  (¾ inch) thick slices
400 g (13 oz) spaghetti
salt and pepper
chopped tarragon leaves,
  to garnish

- Pour the measurement water over the saffron in a heatproof bowl and leave to infuse.

- Heat the butter in a large saucepan, add the fennel and cook over a medium heat for 5 minutes until softened. Pour over the wine and saffron with the soaking liquid and add the mussels. Cover with a lid and cook for 5 minutes until the mussels have opened. Discard any that remain closed. Stir through the crème fraîche and season.

- Meanwhile, heat the oil in a nonstick frying pan, add the monkfish and cook over a high heat for 3 minutes on each side or until just cooked through. Carefully stir the monkfish into the mussel sauce.

- While the mussel sauce is cooking, cook the pasta in a large saucepan of salted boiling water according to the pack instructions until al dente. Drain, reserving a little of the cooking water. Stir through the mussel sauce, adding a little cooking water if needed, and season.

- Spoon into serving bowls and serve sprinkled with the tarragon.

Quick Monkfish Spaghetti Cook the monkfish, as above, under a preheated hot grill for 3–5 minutes on each side. Meanwhile, cook and drain the spaghetti as above. Stir through the monkfish, 1 chopped tomato, ½ chopped red chilli, deseeded if liked, a squeeze of lemon juice and a handful of chopped flat-leaf parsley. Serve immediately.

Spaghetti with Pancetta-wrapped Monkfish Cut a 400 g (13 oz) piece of monkfish in half lengthwise, removing any bone. Lay the two halves on top of each other to make a slab of even thickness, then wrap 8 pancetta slices around to secure the two halves. Cook under a preheated hot grill for 7–10 minutes, then turn over and cook for a further 7–10 minutes or until the fish is just cooked through. Meanwhile, prepare the saffron threads as above and leave to infuse for 10 minutes, then mix together with 50 ml (2 fl oz) double cream. While the saffron is infusing, cook and drain the spaghetti as above. Cut the monkfish into slices, adding any juices to the saffron sauce. Toss the sauce through the drained pasta and serve alongside the fish.

Summery Sausage Pasta

Serves 4

4 tablespoons olive oil

6 large pork sausages

2 onions, sliced

2 red and 2 yellow peppers,
 cored, deseeded and sliced

1 garlic clove, crushed

1 tablespoon tomato purée

2 teaspoons sugar

1 tablespoon balsamic vinegar

3 large tomatoes, chopped

2 tablespoons water

handful of basil leaves, chopped,
 plus extra to garnish

400 g (13 oz) radiatore pasta

salt and pepper

- Grease a baking sheet with 1 tablespoon of the oil, add the sausages and place in a preheated oven, 200°C (400°F), Gas Mark 6, for 20–25 minutes, until brown and cooked through.

- Meanwhile, heat the remaining oil in a saucepan, add the onions and cook for 5 minutes until softened. Add the peppers, garlic, tomato purée, sugar, vinegar, tomatoes and measurement water. Cover and cook for 15 minutes. Remove the lid and cook for a further 5 minutes until the peppers are really soft. Season well and stir through the basil.

- While the sausages and peppers are cooking, cook the pasta in a large saucepan of salted boiling water according to the pack instructions until al dente. Drain, reserving a little of the cooking water, and return to the pan.

- Slice the sausages into bite-sized pieces. Stir through the pasta with the peppers, adding a little cooking water to loosen if needed. Season well. Spoon into serving bowls and serve sprinkled with extra chopped basil.

Winter Sausage Pasta Steam ½ head of thinly sliced cabbage over a saucepan of boiling water for 10 minutes until soft. Meanwhile, cook 400 g (13 oz) fusilli according to the pack instructions until al dente. Drain the pasta and return to the pan. Stir through the cabbage, 3 smoked sausages (such as kielbasa), sliced, a knob of butter and 25 g (1 oz) grated Parmesan cheese. Serve immediately.

Spanish-Style Sausage Pasta Rub 2 tablespoons olive oil over 4 red peppers and cook under a preheated hot grill for 10 minutes, turning frequently, until charred all over. Place in a plastic food bag, seal and leave for 5 minutes. When cooled, peel away the blackened skin. Cut in half, remove the seeds and slice. Meanwhile, cook the radiatore as above. Heat 1 tablespoon olive oil in a frying pan, add 150 g (5 oz) chorizo sausage, cut into chunks, and sizzle for a couple of minutes. Add the sliced peppers and a splash of water, season well and cook for a further few minutes. Drain the pasta and return to the pan. Toss through the chorizo and peppers and serve with shavings of Manchego cheese.

PAS-FOOD-WEO

Seared Sea Bass with Warm Pasta Salad and Basil Oil

Serves 4

2 tablespoons olive oil
4 small sea bass fillets, boned
300 g (10 oz) fregola pasta
squeeze of lemon juice
75 g (3 oz) sun-blush tomatoes
in oil, drained and chopped
50 g (2 oz) pitted black olives
salt and pepper

For the basil oil

100 ml (3½ fl oz) extra virgin
olive oil
large handful of basil leaves,
roughly chopped
1 garlic clove

- To make the basil oil, place the extra virgin olive oil in a small saucepan, add the basil and garlic and cook over a low heat for 10 minutes. Leave to cool, then pass the flavoured oil through a sieve.

- Heat the oil in a large nonstick frying pan, add the sea bass, skin side down, and cook over a high heat for 5–7 minutes until golden and crisp. Carefully turn over, season well and cook for a further 3–5 minutes or until the fish is opaque and cooked through. Slice each fillet in half.

- Meanwhile, cook the pasta in a large saucepan of salted boiling water according to the pack instructions until al dente. Drain well. Stir in 2 tablespoons of the basil oil, a good squeeze of lemon juice, the tomatoes and olives and season.

- Arrange the fish alongside the pasta salad on serving plates and drizzle over the remaining basil oil.

---

1 **Olive and Pesto Pasta with Pan-Fried Sea Bass** Cook the fregole pasta as above. Meanwhile, cut 4 boned sea bass fillets into thin strips and fry in a little olive oil in a frying pan for 3 minutes on each side or until just cooked through. Drain the pasta and return to the pan. Stir through 4 tablespoons shop-bought fresh green pesto and a handful of pitted black olives. Pile the pasta into serving bowls, arrange the fish strips on top and then scatter over 1 chopped tomato. Serve immediately.

3 **Olive and Tomato Pasta with Poached Sea Bass** Put 1 tablespoon red wine vinegar and 1 crushed garlic clove in a bowl, then stir in 5 chopped tomatoes and leave to stand for at least 20 minutes. Meanwhile, chop 1 onion, 1 celery stick and 1 carrot and add to a shallow frying pan with a couple of peppercorns, 1 bay leaf, 1 sliced lemon and about 1 litre (1¾ pints) water. Bring to the boil, then reduce the heat and simmer for 10 minutes. Add 4 boned sea bass fillets, and poach for 10 minutes or until cooked and the fish flakes easily. While the fish is poaching, cook and drain the fregole pasta as above. Remove the skin from the sea bass, break into flakes and add to the pasta with the chopped tomatoes, a handful of chopped basil leaves and a handful of pitted black olives. Serve immediately.

 Fiery Black Spaghetti with Squid

Serves 4

400 g (13 oz) black squid ink
   spaghetti
4 tablespoons olive oil, plus extra
   to serve
400 g (13 oz) prepared squid,
   cleaned and sliced into rings
4 garlic cloves, sliced
1 red chilli, deseeded, if liked,
   and sliced
juice of 1 lemon
handful of basil leaves, chopped
salt and pepper

- Cook the pasta in a large saucepan of salted boiling water according to the pack instructions until al dente.

- Meanwhile, heat the oil in a large frying pan. Pat the squid rings dry with kitchen paper, then add to the pan and cook over a high heat for about 30 seconds until starting to brown. Add the garlic and chilli and cook for a couple of seconds, taking care not to let the garlic burn. The squid should be white and just cooked through. Squeeze over the lemon juice and season to taste.

- Drain the pasta and return to the pan. Toss through the squid and basil, and olive oil to taste. Serve immediately.

2 **Lemony Black Spaghetti with Seared Squid** Heat a little butter in a saucepan, add 1 finely chopped shallot and 3 sliced garlic cloves and cook gently until soft. Squeeze over the juice of 1 lemon, then, over a low heat, whisk in 50 g (2 oz) cold butter, cubed. Sprinkle with a handful of torn basil leaves and set aside. Cook the squid ink spaghetti as above. Cut 8 prepared and cleaned small squid in half. Lightly score each half to make a criss-cross pattern. Toss in a little olive oil and salt. Cook on a preheated hot griddle pan for 2 minutes, turning until charring and curling up. Drain the pasta, toss through the lemon sauce. Serve with the squid and sprinkle with dried chilli flakes and extra chopped basil.

3 **Fiery Black Spaghetti and Seafood Parcels** Parboil the squid ink spaghetti for 5 minutes in a large saucepan of salted boiling water, then drain, cool under cold water and drain again. Meanwhile, fry the chilli and garlic in the oil in a large saucepan as above, pour over 50 ml (2 fl oz) dry white wine and cook for a couple of minutes. Add 4 chopped tomatoes, 150 g (5 oz) cleaned clams and 150 g (5 oz) debearded and cleaned mussels, cover with a lid and cook for a further 5 minutes until the shells have opened. Discard any that remain closed. Add the squid, prepared as above, and spaghetti and season to taste. Divide the mixture between 4 large squares of foil, then lift up the edges and fold over to seal. Place on a baking sheet and cook in a preheated oven, 200°C (400°F) Gas Mark 6, for 10 minutes or until the pasta and squid are cooked through. Tear open with a knife and serve sprinkled with some chopped basil leaves.

Venison and Chestnut Gnocchetti Sardi

Serves 4

1 tablespoon olive oil

6 large venison sausages

1 garlic clove, finely chopped

1 rosemary sprig

1 teaspoon tomato purée

75 ml (3 fl oz) red wine

100 ml (3½ fl oz) hot chicken or
  game stock

100 g (3½ oz) shop-bought
  cooked and peeled
  chestnuts, halved

400 g (13 oz) gnocchetti
  sardi pasta

75 ml (3 fl oz) double cream

salt and pepper

chopped flat-leaf parsley,
  to garnish

- Heat the oil in a pan, add the sausages and cook over a medium heat until golden all over. Remove from the pan, cool slightly and cut into bite-sized pieces. Add the garlic, rosemary and tomato purée to the pan and cook for a couple of minutes, stirring continuously.

- Pour over the wine and bubble until reduced by half. Add the stock, return the sausages to the pan, add the chestnuts and simmer for 20 minutes until the sausages are cooked.

- Meanwhile, cook the pasta in a large saucepan of salted boiling water according to the pack instructions until al dente. Drain, reserving a little of the cooking water, and return to the pan. Add the cream to the sausage sauce and season. Heat through, then stir into the pasta, adding a little cooking water if needed. Spoon into serving bowls and serve sprinkled with the parsley.

---

1 **Fusilli with Chestnut Sauce and Bacon** Cook 400 g (13 oz) fusilli according to the pack instructions until al dente. Meanwhile, cook 4 bacon rashers under a preheated medium grill for 7 minutes or until crisp. Cut into bite-sized pieces. Heat a little olive oil in a frying pan, add 1 chopped garlic clove and cook for 30 seconds. Roughly chop the chestnuts, add the chestnuts, 50 ml (2 fl oz) hot chicken stock and 50 ml (2 fl oz) double cream and simmer for 5 minutes. Drain the pasta and return to the pan, then stir through the chestnut sauce, bacon and a handful of chopped flat-leaf parsley. Serve immediately.

2 **Chicken Liver Pasta** Cut 200 g (7 oz) chicken livers into small pieces, discarding any membrane. Heat a little olive oil in a frying pan, add 2 finely chopped garlic cloves and cook for 30 seconds, then add the chicken livers and cook for a further 3 minutes until golden and just cooked through. Add 75 ml (3 fl oz) dry white wine and cook for a couple of minutes until reduced down. Meanwhile, cook and drain the gnocchetti sardi pasta as above. Stir through the chicken livers and a handful of grated Parmesan cheese. Serve immediately.

Blue Cheese and Cauliflower Cannelloni

Serves 8

1 head of cauliflower, cut into florets
40 g (1½ oz) walnuts
12 fresh lasagne sheets
200 g (7 oz) cream cheese
150 g (5 oz) blue cheese, such as Gorgonzola
oil, for greasing
250 g (8 oz) crème fraîche
5 tablespoons milk
25 g (1 oz) Parmesan cheese, grated
salt and pepper
watercress salad, to serve

- Cook the cauliflower in a saucepan of boiling water for 7–10 minutes until cooked through. Drain loosely and return to the pan. Mash to a rough paste and leave to cool slightly.

- Place the walnuts in a small frying pan and dry-fry for 3 minutes or until lightly golden, then roughly chop. Prepare the lasagne sheets, if necessary, according to the pack instructions.

- Mix together the cooled cauliflower, cream cheese and blue cheese in a bowl. Spoon a little filling along the length of each sheet, then roll up and place in a large greased ovenproof dish.

- Mix together the crème fraîche and milk in a jug until smooth, season and pour over the cannelloni. Scatter with the Parmesan and walnuts.

- Place in a preheated oven, 200°C (400°F), Gas Mark 6, for 10–15 minutes or until golden, bubbling and heated through. Serve with a watercress salad.

Cauliflower Penne with Blue Cheese

Prepare and cook 1 head of cauliflower, as above, and add 500 g (1 lb) fresh penne to the water to cook until al dente. The cauliflower should be just tender and the pasta al dente. Add 200 g (7 oz) baby spinach leaves to the pan just before draining. Drain and return to the pan, then toss together with 150 g (5 oz) chopped blue cheese and a dollop of crème fraîche. Serve.

Cauliflower Pasta and Blue Cheese Soup with Watercress Pesto

Heat a little olive oil in a large saucepan, add the cauliflower, prepared as above, and 1 small chopped onion and cook over a low heat for 5–10 minutes until softened. Pour over 600 ml (1 pint) hot vegetable stock and bring to the boil. Reduce the heat and simmer for 10 minutes. Remove from the heat, then blend together with a stick blender. Return to the heat and add a good dollop of crème fraîche and 100 g (3½ oz) chopped blue cheese. Meanwhile, cook 125 g (4 oz) ditalini according to the pack instructions. Drain, then add to the soup for 1 minute. Place 100 g (3½ oz) watercress, 25 g (1 oz) walnuts, 25 g (1 oz) grated Parmesan cheese and 3 table-spoons extra virgin olive oil in a food processor or blender and whizz together to form a pesto. Ladle the soup into bowls and spoon over the pesto to serve.

Mafaldine with Rich Confit Duck and Pancetta

Serves 4

3 tablespoons olive oil
1 onion, finely chopped
1 carrot, peeled and finely chopped
1 celery stick, finely chopped
1 garlic clove, crushed
1 tablespoon tomato paste
75 ml (3 fl oz) dry white wine
400 g (13 oz) can chopped tomatoes
2 strips of orange peel
200 ml (7 fl oz) water
1 bay leaf
1 thyme sprig
100 g (3½ oz) pancetta cubes
4 confit duck legs
400 g (13 oz) mafaldine
salt and pepper

- Heat 2 tablespoons of the oil in a large saucepan, add the onion, carrot and celery and cook gently for 5 minutes until softened. Stir in the garlic and tomato paste and cook for a further 1 minute.

- Pour over the wine, increase the heat and bubble vigorously for a couple of minutes until reduced, then stir in the tomatoes, orange peel and measurement water. Add the herbs, bring to the boil and cook for 15 minutes.

- Remove the pan from the heat. Remove the orange peel and herbs then, using a stick blender, whizz to form a smooth sauce. Return to the heat.

- Meanwhile, heat the remaining oil in a frying pan, add the pancetta and cook until golden. Using a fork, tear the duck into shreds, then add to the sauce with the pancetta and simmer for 5 minutes.

- While the sauce is cooking, cook the pasta in a large saucepan of salted boiling water according to the pack instructions until al dente. Drain, reserving a little of the cooking water, and return to the pan. Stir through the sauce, adding a little cooking water to loosen if needed. Season to taste and serve immediately.

 Quick Confit Duck and Red Pepper Mafaldine Cook and drain the mafaldine as above. Meanwhile, cut 4 confit duck legs and 2 drained roasted red peppers from a jar into bite-sized pieces. Toss the duck and peppers through the drained pasta with 5 tablespoons crème fraîche and 125 g (4 oz) watercress. Serve immediately.

Easy Confit Duck Mafaldine Pick the meat off 4 confit duck legs. Heat a little olive oil in a frying pan, add the duck and 2 finely chopped garlic cloves and cook over a medium heat for 5 minutes until sizzling. Pour over 50 ml (2 fl oz) dry white wine and 75 ml (3 fl oz) hot chicken stock and cook for 10 minutes until reduced down, then stir in

3 tablespoons crème fraîche. Meanwhile, cook and drain the mafaldine as above, then stir through the sauce and a large handful of chopped rocket leaves. Serve immediately.

Creamy Asparagus Pasta

Serves 4

400 g (13 oz) cappellacci
1 bunch of asparagus, trimmed
15 g (½ oz) butter
1 garlic clove, sliced
150 g (5 oz) mixed wild
    mushrooms, trimmed and
    halved if large
75 g (3 oz) crème fraîche
salt and pepper
Parmesan cheese shavings,
    to serve

· Cook the pasta in a large saucepan of salted boiling water according to the pack instructions until al dente. Add the asparagus 3 minutes before the end of the cooking time and cook until just tender.

· Meanwhile, heat the butter in a frying pan, add the garlic and cook for 1 minute, then stir in the mushrooms and cook for 5 minutes until soft and golden. Stir in the crème fraîche.

· Drain the pasta and asparagus, reserving a little of the cooking water, and return to the pan. Stir through the mushroom sauce and season, adding a little cooking water to loosen if needed. Spoon into serving bowls and serve scattered with the Parmesan shavings.

---

1 Asparagus Linguine with Lemon Carbonara Sauce

Cook 400 g (13 oz) linguine according to the pack instructions until al dente, adding the asparagus as above. Meanwhile, mix together 1 egg, 3 tablespoons crème fraîche and a good squeeze of lemon juice in a bowl. Drain the pasta and asparagus and return to the pan. Toss through the egg sauce and serve immediately.

3 Asparagus and Bacon Pasta Bake

Cook 350 g (11½ oz) penne according to the pack instructions until al dente, adding the asparagus as above. Meanwhile, cook 5 bacon rashers under a preheated medium grill for 10 minutes until cooked through. Cool for 1 minute, then cut into small pieces. Drain the pasta and asparagus and return to the pan. Mix together 150 g (5 oz) soft goats' cheese with enough milk to make a smooth sauce, then stir through the drained pasta with the bacon. Spoon into an ovenproof dish and top with a handful of grated Gruyère cheese. Place in a preheated oven, 200°C (400°F), Gas Mark 6, for 15 minutes or until golden and bubbling.

Linguine with Creamy Marsala Chicken

Serves 4

3 tablespoons olive oil
2 boneless chicken breasts
1 shallot, finely sliced
150 ml (¼ pint) Marsala
150 ml (¼ pint) hot chicken stock
1 sage leaf, finely chopped
100 ml (3½ fl oz) double cream
200 g (7 oz) chestnut
   mushrooms, trimmed and
   halved if large
400 g (13 oz) linguine
salt and pepper
chopped flat-leaf parsley,
   to garnish

- Heat 1 tablespoon of the oil in a frying pan. Season the chicken breasts well and then add to the pan and cook for 5–7 minutes on each side or until golden and cooked through.

- Meanwhile, heat 1 tablespoon of the oil in a saucepan, add the shallot and cook over a low heat for a couple of minutes until softened. Pour over the Marsala, increase the heat to high and cook for a couple of minutes until reduced and slightly syrupy. Add the stock and sage and simmer for a further 5 minutes. Stir in the cream, season well and keep warm.

- Cut the chicken into slices and add to the sauce. Add the remaining oil to the frying pan and cook the mushrooms for 3–5 minutes until golden all over, then stir into the sauce.

- Meanwhile, cook the pasta in a large pan of salted boiling water according to the pack instructions. Drain, reserving a little of the cooking water, and return to the pan. Toss through the sauce, adding cooking water to loosen if needed. Season and serve sprinkled with parsley.

Quick Marsala Chicken Linguine

Cook the linguine as above. Meanwhile, heat a little butter in a frying pan, add 1 chopped garlic clove and cook for 30 seconds. Add the mushrooms as above and cook until golden, then add 2 shop-bought roasted chicken breasts, skin discarded and torn into shreds, and a splash of Marsala and cook for a couple of minutes. Drain the pasta and return to the pan. Toss through the chicken mixture with 4 tablespoons double cream. Serve immediately.

Linguine with Poached Chicken

in Marsala Place 2 boneless, skinless chicken breasts in a pan and pour over 100 ml (3½ fl oz) Marsala and enough chicken stock to cover, then poach gently for 15 minutes or until just cooked through. Meanwhile, cook and drain the linguine and fry the mushrooms as above. Cut the chicken into strips and stir through the drained pasta with the mushrooms, a little of the poaching liquid (boiled down if liked) to loosen and some double cream. Serve at once.

30 Macaroni Prawn Gratin

Serves 6

3 egg yolks
juice of 1 lemon
200 g (7 oz) butter, melted
100 ml (3½ fl oz) double cream
625 g (1¼ lb) macaroni
3 tablespoons olive oil
3 leeks, trimmed, cleaned
   and sliced
300 g (10 oz) large cooked
   peeled prawns
salt and pepper

- Place the egg yolks in a heatproof bowl that will snugly fit over a saucepan of simmering water (make sure the bottom of the bowl doesn't touch the water). Add most of the lemon juice then, very slowly, start to pour in the butter, whisking continuously. As the butter thickens the sauce, you can add it a little quicker. When the sauce has thickened and is the consistency of mayonnaise, remove from the pan. Leave to cool, season well and add more lemon juice to taste. Whip the cream until soft peaks form, then carefully fold into the sauce.

- Meanwhile, cook the pasta in a large saucepan of salted boiling water according to the pack instructions until al dente.

- Heat the oil in a saucepan, add the leeks with a splash of water and cook gently for about 7 minutes until beginning to soften. Add the prawns and cook for 2 minutes or until heated through.

- Drain the pasta and return to the pan, then mix through the sauce, leeks and prawns and season. Spoon into individual gratin dishes and cook under a preheated hot grill for 3–5 minutes or until lightly browned all over.

---

1 Quick Prawn and Leek Pasta Cook the leeks and prawns as above. Meanwhile, cook 625 g (1¼ lb) chifferi according to the pack instructions until al dente. Drain and return to the pan. Stir through the prawn mixture, 5 tablespoons crème fraîche and a good squeeze of lemon juice. Serve sprinkled with chopped basil.

---

2 Tropical Prawn Fusilli Heat a little olive oil in a large frying pan, add 1 chopped garlic clove and ½ deseeded and chopped red chilli and cook for 30 seconds until golden. Add 3 leeks, trimmed, cleaned and sliced, and cook for 5 minutes more. Pour over a 400 g (13 oz) can chopped tomatoes and 100 ml (3½ fl oz) hot vegetable or fish stock, then cook for 10 minutes until softened and reduced. Add the grated rind and juice of 1 lime and 100 ml (3½ fl oz) double cream. Simmer for a further 1–2 minutes, then add 300 g (10 oz) large cooked peeled prawns and heat through. Meanwhile, cook 625 g (1¼ lb) fusilli according to the pack instructions until al dente. Drain and return to the pan, then toss through the sauce with a handful of chopped basil leaves.

Pasta with Salmon, Rocket and Red Onion

Serves 4

400 g (13 oz) casareccia pasta
100 ml (3½ fl oz) dry white wine
150 ml (¼ pint) double cream
250 g (8 oz) smoked salmon,
  cut into strips
75 g (3 oz) rocket leaves
½ red onion, thinly sliced
grated rind of ½ lemon
2 teaspoons capers, rinsed
  and drained
salt and pepper

· Cook the pasta in a large saucepan of salted boiling water according to the pack instructions until al dente.

· Meanwhile, heat the wine in a saucepan until boiling, then reduce the heat and simmer for 5 minutes. Stir through the cream, season and leave to bubble for a couple of minutes.

· Drain the pasta, reserving a little of the cooking water, and return to the pan. Stir through the sauce, adding a little cooking water to loosen if needed. Toss through the remaining ingredients and serve immediately.

Salmon, Red Onion and Rocket Pasta Salad Cook 300 g (10 oz) orzo according to the pack instructions. Drain, then cool under cold running water and drain again. Meanwhile, mix together 2 tablespoons natural yogurt, 4 tablespoons mayonnaise and plenty of black pepper in a bowl. Tip the pasta into a serving dish and stir through the yogurt with the smoked salmon, rocket, onion, lemon rind and capers as above.

Pasta with Honey-Roasted Salmon Drizzle 1 tablespoon honey and a good grinding of black pepper over 2 thick salmon fillets. Place in a preheated oven, 200°C (400°F), Gas Mark 6, for 12–15 minutes or until the fish is cooked through and flakes easily. Meanwhile, cook the casareccia pasta as above. Heat a little olive oil in a frying pan, add 1 chopped red onion and cook until softened, then pour over 75 ml (3 fl oz) dry white wine and simmer until reduced. Add 1 teaspoon Dijon mustard, the grated rind of ½ lemon and 75 ml (3 fl oz) double cream and heat through. Drain the pasta and return to the pan. Remove any skin and bones from the salmon, then flake and add to the sauce. Toss the sauce through the drained pasta with 75 g (3 oz) rocket leaves and serve immediately.

Creamy Lobster Fettuccine

Serves 2

25 g (1 oz) butter
2 shallots, finely chopped
1 teaspoon tomato purée
1 large cooked lobster
2 tablespoons brandy
150 ml (¼ pint) Madeira
75 ml (3 fl oz) double cream
1 egg yolk
pinch of cayenne pepper
200 g (7 oz) fettuccine
salt and pepper
chopped tarragon leaves,
  to garnish

- Heat the butter in a large frying pan, add the shallots and cook over a low heat until softened. Stir in the tomato purée and cook for 1 minute. Meanwhile, remove the lobster meat from the shell and cut the tails in half. Add the lobster shell to the frying pan and cook for 5–10 minutes until browned.

- Remove the pan from the heat and add the brandy. Return to the heat and boil vigorously until reduced down. Pour over the Madeira and bubble for 5–10 minutes until reduced by half. Pass through a sieve, pressing down hard to extract the juices.

- Return the sauce to the pan. Mix together the cream, egg yolk and cayenne pepper. Add a tablespoon of the sauce to the cream mixture to warm a little, then stir the cream into the pan. Heat through but do not let it boil, then add the lobster meat.

- Meanwhile, cook the pasta in a large saucepan of salted boiling water according to the pack instructions until al dente. Drain, reserving a little of the cooking water, and return to the pan. Toss the sauce through the pasta until coated all over, adding a little cooking water to loosen if needed, and season.

- Spoon into serving bowls, top with the lobster tail and serve sprinkled with the tarragon.

Quick Lobster Fettuccine Cook the fettuccine as above. Drain, reserving a little of the cooking water, and return to the pan. Stir through 200 g (7 oz) potted lobster, 1 egg yolk and a handful of chopped tarragon leaves and serve immediately.

Lobster Pasta Salad Cook 200 g (7 oz) orzo according to the pack instructions. Drain, then cool under cold running water and drain again. Stir together 3 tablespoons mayonnaise, 3 tablespoons soured cream, the grated rind and juice of ½ lemon, 1 finely chopped shallot and a handful of chopped chives and tarragon in a bowl. Stir in the chopped lobster meat from 1 cooked lobster. Tip the pasta into a serving dish and toss together with the lobster mixture and a large handful of rocket leaves.

Pappardelle with Chestnuts, Rocket and Parma Ham

Serves 4

75 ml (3 fl oz) olive oil, plus extra
to serve
6 sage leaves
rind of ½ lemon, cut into strips
100 g (3½ oz) shop-bought
cooked and peeled chestnuts,
halved if liked
400 g (13 oz) pappardelle
juice of ½ lemon
50 g (2 oz) rocket leaves
150 g (5 oz) Parma ham
salt and pepper

- Place the oil in a medium-sized pan, add the sage leaves and lemon rind and heat very gently for about 10 minutes. Add the chestnuts and cook gently for a further 10 minutes. Remove from the heat and set aside for 10 minutes.

- Meanwhile, cook the pasta in a large saucepan of salted boiling water according to the pack instructions until al dente. Drain.

- Remove the lemon rind and sage leaves from the oil. Toss together the chestnut lemon oil with the pasta.

- Pile on to serving plates and arrange the rocket and Parma ham on top. Serve immediately with a squeeze of lemon juice over each portion.

Simple Parma Ham and Chestnut Pappardelle Cook and drain the pappardelle as above. Meanwhile, heat a little olive oil in a frying pan, add the Parma ham and cook until sizzling. Remove from the pan and add the chestnuts, prepared as above, and 1 sliced garlic clove. Cook for a further 3 minutes until golden. Squeeze over the juice and grated rind of 1 lemon, then toss through the drained pasta with the Parma ham, broken into small pieces. Serve sprinkled with chopped flat-leaf parsley.

Creamy Chestnut and Mushroom Pappardelle Soak 25 g (1 oz) porcini mushrooms in a little boiling water for 15 minutes or until soft. Meanwhile, heat a little butter in a frying pan, add 1 chopped shallot and cook gently until softened. Pour over 50 ml (2 fl oz) Marsala and bubble until reduced. Add 150 ml (¼ pint) hot chicken stock and the chestnuts, prepared as above, and simmer for 10 minutes until softened. While the sauce is cooking, cook and drain the pappardelle as above. Stir the mushrooms and soaking liquid into the sauce, cook for a further couple of minutes, then add 50 ml (2 fl oz) double cream and toss through the drained pasta and top with Parma ham.

Creamy Tomato Pasta with Prawns

Serves 4

25 g (1 oz) butter
1 onion, finely chopped
1 celery stick, finely chopped
1 garlic clove, finely chopped
1 teaspoon fennel seeds
150 ml (¼ pint) dry white wine
1 tablespoon brandy
400 g (13 oz) can chopped
    tomatoes
1 thyme sprig
1 bay leaf
50 ml (2 fl oz) double cream
400 g (13 oz) cannelli pasta
1 tablespoon olive oil
8 large raw unpeeled prawns
salt and pepper
chopped basil leaves, to garnish

· Heat the butter in a saucepan, add the onion, celery and garlic and cook over a low heat for 5 minutes or until softened. Add the fennel and cook for a further 30 seconds.

· Remove from the heat, then pour over the wine and brandy. Return to the heat and cook over a high heat for a couple of minutes until reduced down, then add the tomatoes and herbs and simmer for 15–20 minutes, adding a little water if needed.

· Remove the pan from the heat. Discard the herbs, then using a stick blender, whizz to form a smooth sauce. Stir through the cream and season. Meanwhile, cook the pasta in a large saucepan of salted boiling water according to the pack instructions until al dente.

· Heat the oil in a large frying pan, add the prawns and cook for 3 minutes on each side or until pink and cooked through.

· Drain the pasta, reserving a little of the cooking water. Toss through the sauce, adding a little cooking water to loosen if needed. Spoon into bowls and top with the prawns. Serve sprinkled with the basil.

Simple Prawn and Tomato Spaghetti

Cook 400 g (13 oz) spaghetti according to the pack instructions until al dente. Meanwhile, cook the prawns as above under a preheated hot grill for about 3–5 minutes or until they turn pink and are cooked through. Drain the pasta and return to the pan. Stir through the prawns, 50 g (2 oz) garlic butter, 2 chopped tomatoes and the grated rind of 1 lemon. Serve immediately.

Prawn and Tomato Pasta

Heat a little olive oil in a large frying pan, add 1 teaspoon fennel seeds and 2 sliced garlic cloves and cook for 30 seconds. Add 400 g (13 oz) halved baby plum tomatoes, a splash of dry white wine and a little water and simmer for 10 minutes. Stir through the prawns as above and cook for 3–5 minutes or until they turn pink and are cooked through, then stir in 50 g (2 oz) mascarpone cheese. Meanwhile, cook and drain the cannelli pasta as above. Stir through the prawn sauce with a handful of chopped basil leaves. Serve immediately.

Tagliarelle with Seared Steak and Goulash Sauce

Serves 4

2 tablespoons olive oil
1 onion, thinly sliced
1 red pepper, cored, deseeded and chopped
1 tablespoon smoked paprika
400 g (13 oz) can chopped tomatoes
2 thick beef steaks
325 g (11 oz) tagliarelle
50 ml (2 fl oz) soured cream
salt and pepper

- Heat 1 tablespoon of the oil in a large saucepan, add the onion and cook gently for a couple of minutes until softened. Stir in the red pepper and cook for a further 5 minutes until softened. Add the paprika and tomatoes, then season well. Bring to the boil, reduce the heat and simmer for 15 minutes.

- Meanwhile, heat a griddle pan until smoking hot. Rub the remaining oil over the beef steaks and season well. Add to the pan and cook for 2–4 minutes on each side, depending on how you like your meat cooked. Leave to rest for 5 minutes and cut into bite-sized pieces.

- Cook the pasta in a large saucepan of salted boiling water according to the pack instructions until al dente. Drain, reserving a little of the cooking water, and return to the pan.

- Stir the chopped steak and half of the soured cream into the tomato sauce, then mix into the pasta, adding a little cooking water to loosen if needed. Pile the pasta on to serving plates and dollop over the remaining cream. Serve.

 Quick Stir-Fried Beef and Red Pepper Tagliarelle Heat a little olive oil in a wok or large frying pan, add 1 chopped garlic clove and 300 g (10 oz) stir-fry beef strips and stir-fry for a minute or two, then add a pinch of dried chilli flakes, 125 g (4 oz) halved cherry tomatoes and 1 drained, chopped roast red pepper from a jar. Add a splash of water and cook over a high heat until cooked through. Meanwhile, cook and drain the tagliarelle as above. Toss through the beef mixture. Top with natural yogurt.

 Tagliarelle with Seared Steak and Pizzaiola Sauce Heat a little olive oil in a frying pan, add 300 g (10 oz) sirloin steak and cook over a high heat for 5 minutes until browned all over. Remove from the pan and leave to rest. Add a 400 g (13 oz) can chopped tomatoes, 1 crushed garlic clove, 1 teaspoon dried oregano and a handful of pitted black olives to the pan and bubble for about 10 minutes until thickened. Meanwhile, cook and drain the tagliarelle as above. Cut the steak into slices, stir through the sauce and then add to the drained pasta. Serve immediately.

Sweet Potato Pockets with Sage Butter and Amaretti

Serves 4

1 freshly rolled large fresh
  pasta sheet, or 24 gyoza or
  wonton wrappers
flour, for dusting
1 egg yolk, for brushing
2 amaretti biscuits, crumbled

For the filling

3 small sweet potatoes, peeled
  and chopped
40 g (1½ oz) Parmesan cheese,
  grated
grating of nutmeg
salt and pepper

For the sage butter

50 g (2 oz) butter
8 sage leaves

- To make the filling, cook the sweet potato in a large saucepan of boiling water for 10 minutes or until just soft, then drain well. Leave to cool slightly, then mix together with the cheese and nutmeg in a bowl and season to taste.

- Lay the pasta sheet on a clean work surface lightly dusted with flour, then cut out 12 x 3 cm (1 inch) squares and 12 x 4 cm (1½ inch) squares. Alternatively, use gyoza or wonton wrappers. Place a heaped tablespoon of filling in the centre of a smaller square or wrapper, then brush a little egg around the edges. Lightly brush the edges of the larger squares or wrapper with egg and place over the filling. Gently press out any excess air and then use your fingers to seal. Place on a baking sheet lightly dusted with flour. Repeat with the remaining squares or wrappers and filling.

- Cook the pasta in two batches in a large saucepan of salted boiling water for 3 minutes. Drain, reserving a little of the cooking water.

- To make the sage butter, heat the butter in a small frying pan until it foams. Add the sage leaves and cook for a minute, then whisk in 3–4 tablespoons of the cooking water to form a sauce. Arrange the pasta on plates and drizzle over the sauce. Serve sprinkled with the amaretti biscuits.

---

1 Easy Sweet Potato and Sage Penne

Cook the sweet potato as above, adding 400 g (13 oz) penne to the pan and cooking until al dente. Drain and return to the pan, then toss through a handful of chopped sage leaves, 25 g (1 oz) butter and 25 g (1 oz) grated Parmesan cheese. Serve immediately.

2 Sweet Potato and Almond Penne

Cut 2 peeled sweet potatoes into chunks and brush with olive oil. Cook under a preheated medium grill for 10 –15 minutes or until browned and soft. Meanwhile, cook 400 g (13 oz) penne according to the pack instructions until al dente. Place 100 g (3½ oz) almonds and 50 ml (2 fl oz) water in a food processor or blender and whizz together to form a paste. Heat 25 g (1 oz) butter in a frying pan, add the paste and cook for 3–5 minutes until thickened. Add 25 g (1 oz) grated Parmesan cheese and a squeeze of lemon juice and heat through. Drain the pasta and return to the pan, then stir through the almond sauce and sweet potatoes. Serve immediately.

Index

Page references in *italics* indicate photographs.

Acknowledgements

Executive editor: Eleanor Maxfield
Editor: Joanne Wilson
Copy-editor: Jo Murray
Art Director: Jonathan Christie
Design: www.gradedesign.com
Art Direction: Juliette Norsworthy & Tracy Killick
Photographer: Craig Robertson
Home economist: Emma Lewis
Stylist: Isabel De Cordova